Family Ties In England, Scotland, Wales, & Ireland

Family Ties In England, Scotland, Wales, & Ireland

Sources For
Genealogical Research

Compiled by
Judith P. Reid
Humanities and Social Sciences Division

Library of Congress Washington 1998

LIBRARY OF CONGRESS CATALOGING-IN-PUBLICATION DATA

Reid, Judith P.
    Family ties in England, Scotland, Wales, and Ireland :
    sources for genealogical research / compiled by Judith P.
    Reid.
            p.   8cm.
        Includes bibliographical references and index.
        ISBN 0–8444–0911–1
        1. Great Britain—Genealogy—Bibliography—Catalogs. 2.
    Great Britain—Genealogy—Manuscripts—Catalogs. 3. Library
    of Congress—Catalogs. I. Title.
    Z5313.G69R45   1998
    [CS414]   96–42143
    016.929'1'072041—dc20   CIP

For sale by the U.S. Government Printing Office, Superintendent of Documents,
Mail Stop: SSOP, Washington, DC 20402–9328   ISBN 0–8444–0911–1

Contents

Introduction

his guide has been prepared as an aid for the many researchers who come to the Library of Congress's Local History and Genealogy Room to research family roots in England, Ireland, Scotland, or Wales. The Library's collection of local history and genealogical material for the British Isles and Ireland is so large that it ranks second only to the Library's holdings of materials relating to the United States. This should not be surprising, as British local history societies have pursued active publishing programs since the 1700s and have produced hundreds of parish registers and other local records; the Library of Congress holds many of these publications.

Researchers have a myriad of reasons for coming to the Library of Congress, such as: reading already published genealogies, learning more about how to do British Isles genealogical research, building on research begun elsewhere by using the Library's extensive holdings of scholarly British local history publications, checking facts and culling biographical information, seeking information about the origin of family names, identifying geographic areas where families lived, or researching clans and tartans. Confronting this wide range of information can be daunting to the beginner. This book was prepared to assist would-be users of the British Isles collections—beginners or experienced users alike—to access these materials.

While this guide has been prepared primarily as an aid to researching English, Irish, Scottish, and Welsh genealogy and local history at the Library of Congress, it will also be useful for those searching these subjects in other large libraries. However, it is not intended to be a comprehensive guide to British Isles resources and should be supplemented by P. William Filby's *American & British Genealogy & Heraldry: A Selected List of Books* (Z5311.F55 1983) and supplements.

Nobility and heraldry are other topics of frequent interest. However, because relatively few Americans can trace their British Isles or Irish ancestry to royalty and nobility, these topics were deemed to be beyond the scope of this guide. Similarly, heraldry, a worthy subject in its own right, is beyond the basic needs of most individuals who are beginning to examine their British ancestry.

The overall arrangement of this guide is by subject. Although the contents for each country vary somewhat, the following basic subjects will be found for each: Handbooks, providing assistance for beginning research; Pedigrees and Family Histories, highlighting published genealogies; Bibliographies, listing sources for further research; Local History, detailing a myriad of references to information about places; Biographical Information, citing personal and professional details about ancestors in all disciplines; Maps, Atlases, Gazetteers, showing the location and giving an account of the historical development of areas; Names, Geographical, defining the origin and history of places; Names, Personal, discussing the origins and locations of family names; and Periodicals, identifying major journals and magazines on the subject. Supplementing these are unique subject headings for individual countries, such as Clans and Tartans for Scotland. The contents are supplemented by the Author and Title Index.

While the book is divided into four distinctive sections highlighting specific resources available for researching English, Irish, Scottish, or Welsh genealogy, in practice the records and the published materials are not always so clearly segmented. The research material reflects the interwoven historical development of these cultures and countries. Reflecting these complex relationships, some citations may be duplicated in several parts of this book, while others, which only appear in one section, may be useful in all four subject areas.

Coats of arms and badges borne by the Neville Family of England. Illustrated in *Histories of Noble British Families with Bibliographical Notices of the Most Distinguished Individuals in Each* by Henry Drummond, London: William Pickering, 1846, CS419.D7 1846 folio, vol. 2, p. 28 in back of book, oppos. table 7. Library of Congress.

Chapter One

Sources for Research in English Genealogy

CONTENTS

Handbooks

1.
Baxter, Angus, 1912–
In search of your British & Irish roots : a complete guide to tracing your English, Welsh, Scottish & Irish ancestors / Angus Baxter.—Rev. and updated.—Baltimore : Genealogical Pub. Co., 1989—x, 310 p. : ill. CS414.B38 1989
Includes bibliographical references (p. 302–306).

2.
Bethell, David.
English ancestry / by David Bethell ; maps by Irene Margaret Barron.—Leek, Staffordshire, England : Melandra, c1981.—vii, 387 p. : ill. CS414.B47

3.
Cole, Jean A., 1944–
Tracing your family tree : the complete guide to discovering your family history / Jean A. Cole and Michael Armstrong.—Hammersmith, London : Thorson, 1990.—208 p. : ill. CS414.C63 1990

4.
Currer-Briggs, Noel.
Debrett's family historian : a guide to tracing your ancestry / Noel Currer-Briggs and Royston Gambier ; introduction by Sir Iain Moncreiffe ; foreword by Lord Teviot.—London : Debrett Webb & Bower, 1981.—208 p. : ill. CS414.C87 1981

5.
FitzHugh, Terrick V. H.
The dictionary of genealogy / Terrick V. H. FitzHugh. 4th ed. / Revised by Susan Lumas on behalf of the Society of Genealogists. London : A & C Black, 1994.—304 p. : ill., maps. CS6.F58 1994

Includes bibliographical references.

6.
FitzHugh, Terrick V. H.
How to write a family history : the lives and times of our ancestors / Terrick V. H. FitzHugh.—Sherborne, Dorset : Alphabooks ; London : A & C Black, 1988.—200 p. : ill. CS14.F57 1988
"Sources & Records": p. 195–197.

7.

Gardner, David E.

Genealogical research in England and Wales / [by] David E. Gardner [and] Frank Smith ; artwork by Mariel P. Gardner.— Salt Lake City : Bookcraft Publishers, c1956–1964.—3 v. : ill., port., maps, forms, tables.   **CS414.G3**

Includes bibliographical footnotes.

8.

Hamilton-Edwards, Gerald Kenneth Savery, 1906–

In search of army ancestry / by Gerald Hamilton-Edwards.— London : Phillimore, 1977.—106 p. : ill.   **CS415.H36**

Bibliography: p. 96–99.

9.

Hamilton-Edwards, Gerald Kenneth Savery.

In search of British ancestry / Gerald Hamilton-Edwards.—4th ed.—Baltimore : Genealogical Pub. Co., 1983.—ix, 212 p. : ill.
                                                       CS414.H35 1983

Bibliography: p. 176–205.

10.

Hey, David.

The Oxford guide to family history / David Hey.—Oxford ; New York : Oxford University Press, 1993.—x, 246 p. : ill., (some col.), maps.   **CS9.H49 1993**

Includes bibliographical references (p. 231–236) and indexes.

11.

Holding, Norman H.

More sources of World War I army ancestry / Norman Holding.—2nd ed.—Birmingham, England : Federation of Family History Societies, 1991.—88 p. : ill.   **CS415.H65 1991**

Includes bibliographical references (p. 85).

12.

Irvine, Sherry.

Your English ancestry : a guide for North Americans / by Sherry Irvine.—Salt Lake City : Ancestry, c1993.— ix, 196 p. : ill., maps.   **CS415.I78 1993**

Includes bibliographical references (p. [171]–185) and index.

13.

Kitzmiller, John M. (John Michael), 1953–

In search of the "forlorn hope" : a comprehensive guide to locating British regiments and their records (1640–WWI) / by John M. Kitzmiller, II.—Salt Lake City, Utah : Manuscript Pub. Foundation, c1988.—2 v. (xx, 1583 p., 28 p. of plates : ill.; + 1 suppl. (viii, 268 p.).   **UA649.K56 1988**

Includes bibliographical references (v. 2, p. 1519–1527).

14.

Mellen, Rachael.
The handy book to English genealogy / by Rachael Mellen.—
3rd ed., rev. and expanded.—Bowie, Md. : Heritage Books,
1990.—x, 218 p. : ill.   **CS414.M45 1990**
Rev. ed. of: *A Practical Guide for the Genealogist in England.*
2nd ed., rev. and expanded, 1987.
Includes bibliographical references (p. 187) and index.

15.

The Oxford companion to local and family history / edited by
David Hey.—New York : Oxford University Press, 1996.—
517 p.   **CS9.O94 1996**

16.

Rogers, Colin Darlington.
Tracing your English ancestors : a manual for analysing and
solving genealogical problems, 1538 to the present / Colin D.
Rogers.—1st USA ed.—Manchester, UK ; New York :
Manchester University Press ; New York ; Distributed in the
USA and Canada by St. Martin's Press, 1989.—x, 182 p.
                                                         CS414.R64 1989
Rev. ed. of: *The Family Tree Detective,* 1985.
Includes bibliographical references (p. [156]–159) and index.

17.

Saul, Pauline A.
The A–Z guide to tracing ancestors in Britain / Pauline Saul &
F. C. Markwell.—4th ed.—Baltimore : Genealogical Pub. Co.,
1991.—256 p. : ill., maps.   **CS414.M37 1991**

18.

Steel, D. J. (Donald John).
Discovering your family history / by Don Steel ; edited by Bryn
Brooks.—Rev. ed.—London : British Broadcasting Corp.,
1986.—195 p.   **CS414.S74 1986**
Bibliography: p. 168–191.

19.

Wagner, Anthony Richard, *Sir.*
English genealogy / Sir Anthony Wagner.—3rd ed.—
Chichester, Sussex : Phillimore, 1983.—xii, 475 p. : geneal.
tables.   **CS414 .W3 1983**
Includes bibliographical references and index.

20.

Willis, Arthur James.
Genealogy for beginners / Arthur J. Willis and Molly Tatchell.—
5th ed. rev.—Chichester, Sussex, England : Phillimore, 1984.—
200 p. : ill.   **CS16 .W55 1984**
Bibliography: p. [103]–109.

21.

Yurdan, Marilyn.

 Tracing your ancestors / Marilyn Yurdan.—Newton Abbot :
David & Charles, 1988.—192 p. : ill.   **CS414.Y87 1988**

  Includes bibliographical references (p. 188–190) and index.

Pedigrees &
Family Histories

22.

Barrow, Geoffrey Battiscombe.

 The genealogist's guide : an index to printed British pedigrees
and family histories, 1950–1975 / compiled by Geoffrey B.
Barrow ; with a foreword by Anthony J. Camp.—London :
Research Pub. Co. ; Chicago : American Library Association,
1977.—xv, 205 p.   **Z5313.G69 B36 1977**

  "Being a supplement to G. W. Marshall's *Genealogists guide*
and J.B. Whitmore's *Genealogical guide*."—t.p.

23.

Bridger, Charles, 1825 or 6–1879.

 An index to printed pedigrees contained in county and local
histories, the Herald's visitations and in the more important
genealogical collections / by Charles Bridger.—London : J. R.
Smith, 1867.—iv, 384 p.   **Microfilm 481552**

  Reprinted in Baltimore by Genealogical Pub. Co. in 1969.
    (Z5313.G69 B8 1969)

24.

Marshall, George W. (George William), 1839–1905.

 The genealogist's guide / by George W. Marshall.—Guildford :
priv. print for the author by Billing and sons, 1903.—xiii, 880 p.
    Z5313.G69 M42

  Reprinted with a new introduction by Anthony J. Camp in
Baltimore by Genealogical Pub. Co. in 1967 and 1973.

25.

Norr, Vernon M., 1898–

 Some early English pedigrees : combined from most available
sources, 1958–1968 / by Vernon M. Norr.—[Arlington, Va., :
s.n., 1968].—148 leaves.   **CS438 .N6**

26.

Thomson, T. R. (Theodore Radford), 1897–

 A catalogue of British family histories / compiled by T. R.
Thomson ; with an introduction by Lord Farrer.—3rd ed.—
London : Research Pub. Co. [for] the Society of Genealogists,

1976.—184 p.   **Z5313.G69 T4 1976**
    Updated by the Society of Genealogists, London.

27.

Whitmore, John Beach.
    A genealogical guide : an index to British pedigrees in continuation of Marshall's Genealogists's guide (1903).—London : Sold by Walford Bros., 1953.—xxxvii, 658 p.   **Z5313.G69 W45 1953**

Bibliographies

28.

Filby, P. William.
    American & British genealogy & heraldry : a selected list of books / compiled by P. William Filby.—3rd ed.—Boston : New England Historic Genealogical Society, 1983.—xix, 736 p.
    Z5311.F55 1983

——— ——— Supplement, 1982–1985.—Boston : New England Historic Genealogical Society, 1987.—xvii, 230 p.
    Z5311.F55 1983 Suppl

29.

Gatfield, George.
    Guide to printed books and manuscripts relating to English and foreign heraldry and genealogy / by George Gatfield.—London : Mitchell & Hughes, 1892.—2 leaves, 646 p.   **Z5311.G26**
    Reprinted in Detroit by Gale Research Co. in 1966.

30.

Humphery-Smith, Cecil R.
    A genealogist's bibliography / Cecil R. Humphery-Smith.—[New ed.].—Baltimore : Genealogical Pub. Co., 1985.—128 p.
    Z5313.G69 H84 1985
    Bibliography: p. 114–128.

31.

Kaminkow, Marion J.
    A new bibliography of British genealogy with notes.—Baltimore : Magna Carta Book Co., 1965.—xvii, 170 p.
    Z5313.G69 K3

32.

Mullins, E. L. C. (Edward Lindsay Carson).
    A guide to the historical and archaeological publications of societies in England and Wales, 1901–1933 / compiled for the Institute of Historical Research [by] E. L. C. Mullins.—London : Athlone Press, 1968.—xiii, 850 p.   **Z5055.G6 M8**

33.

Mullins, E. L. C. (Edward Lindsay Carson).

Texts and calendars : an analytical guide to serial publications.—
London : Royal Historical Society, 1958.—xi, 674 p.—(Royal
Historical Society [London], Guides and Handbooks ; no. 7).

Z2016.M8

"An analytical guide to printed texts and calendars relating
to English and Welsh history issued in general collections or
in series by a public body or private society before the end of
March 1957. The volumes . . . [described] are, with few excep-
tions, part of the Library of the Royal Historical Society."

34.

Mullins, E. L. C. (Edward Lindsay Carson).

Texts and calendars II : an analytical guide to serial publications,
1957–1982 / by E. L. C. Mullins.—London : Offices of the
Royal Historical Society, University College London, 1983.—
xi, 323 p.—(Royal Historical Society guides and handbooks ;
no. 12).   **Z2016.M82 1983**

Parish Registers

Parish registers are church records that document births, marriages, and
deaths. They exist in three forms: published alone, published as part of
a local history series, and unpublished. Registers published as indepen-
dent monographs can be identified in a library's catalogs; consultation
with a reference librarian may be helpful. Registers that are published as
part of a local history society series may be identified through use of the
three Mullins guides listed above. Locations of unpublished parish
records may be identified in the works listed below.

35.

Guildhall Library (London, England).

A handlist of parish registers, register transcripts, and related
records at Guildhall Library.—6th (rev.) ed.—London :
Guildhall Library, 1990– . v. <1>.—(Guildhall Library research
guide ; 4).   **CD1068.L6G85 1990**

Contents: pt. 1. City of London—

36.

The Phillimore atlas and index of parish registers / edited by
Cecil R. Humphery-Smith.—Chichester, Sussex, England :
Phillimore, 1984.—1 atlas (v., 281 p.) : maps (some col.).

G1816.E42 P5 1984 <G&M>

Also published in Baltimore by Genealogical Pub. Co. in 1984.
Shows pre-1832 parochial boundaries.

37.
Society of Genealogists (Great Britain).
Parish register copies in the Library of the Society of Genealogists.
10th ed. London : The Society, 1992.—vi, 120 p.
Z5313.G69 S62 1992

Library sources; no. 1.

38.
Steel, D. J. (Donald John).
National index of parish registers. Edited by D. J. Steel and Mrs.
A. E. F. Steel. London : Society of Genealogists, 1966–<1996>.
v. <1–5, v. 6, pts. 1–5; v. 7; v.8, pts. 1–2; v.9, pts. 1–5; v. 10, pt. 1;
v. 11, pt. 1; v. 12; in 16>.
CD1068.A2 S8
Vol. 3 has imprint : London, Published for the Society of
Genealogists {by} Phillimore. Some volumes have subtitle: A
guide to Anglican, Roman Catholic, and Nonconformist registers before 1837, together with information on marriage licenses, bishop's transcripts, and modern copies.
Stamped on t.p. of v. 5: Magna Carta Book Co., Baltimore, Md.
Contents: v. 1. General sources of births, marriages and
deaths before 1837, v. 2. Sources for nonconformist genealogy
and family history, v. 3. Sources for Roman Catholic genealogy
and family history...Index to Vol. 1–3, v. 4. South East England,
Kent, Surrey and Sussex, v. 5. South Midlands and Welsh border comprising the counties of Gloucestershire, Herefordshire,
Oxfordshire, Shropshire, Warwickshire, and Worcestershire, v.
6. The North and East Midlands, pt. 1, Staffordshire, pt. 2,
Nottinghamshire, pt. 3, Leicestershire and Rutland, pt. 4,
Lincolnshire, pt. 5, Derbyshire, v. 7. East Anglia,
Cambridgeshire, Norfolk, Suffolk, v. 8. The West of England,
pt. 1, Berkshire, pt. 2, Wiltshire, v. 9. Home Counties (north of
the Thames) and South East Midlands, pt. 1, Bedfordshire,
Huntingdonshire, pt. 2, Northamptonshire, pt. 3,
Buckinghamshire, pt. 4. Essex, pt. 5, London and Middlesex,
v. 10. pt. 1, Cheshire, v. 11. North East England, pt. 1, Durham
and Norththumberland, v. 12, Sources for Scottish genealogy
and family history.

39.
Tallis, J. A.
Original parish registers in record offices and libraries / [com-
piled by J. A. Tallis].—Matlock : "Local Population Studies"
[for] the Cambridge Group for the History of Population and
Social Structure, 1974.—128 p.
CD1068.A2 T27

———— ———— First supplement.—1976.—60 p.
CD1068.A2 T27 Suppl.

40.
Timmons, Sylvia A.
Printed English and Welsh parish registers in the George
Peabody Branch, Enoch Pratt Free Library, Baltimore,
Maryland / compiled by Sylvia A. Timmons.—[Baltimore ?] :
S. A. Timmons, [1979].—[104] leaves.
Z7778.G7 T55 1979

Parish Registers on Microfilm

The Challen Parish Register Typescripts (microfilm 23963) include parishes in London, the Midlands, and the southern counties. At the Library of Congress, indexes and lists of additional parish records may be examined in the Microform Reading Room. The MicRR guide No. 50 (also microfiche 2282) indexes the Challen Typescripts and provides a list of additional parish registers available on microfilm in the room. Card catalogs in the Microform Reading Room list holdings for microfilm of British parish registers. The subject heading is "Parish registers."

Boyd's Marriage Index on Microfiche

Boyd's Marriage Index, begun by Percival Boyd in the 1920s and covering the period 1538 to 1837, was compiled from English parish registers, bishops' transcripts, and marriage licenses in sixteen counties. Since only about one third of the parishes are represented in this compilation it is incomplete, having less than sixteen percent of all English marriages for that period. The microfilm publication consists of three parts: *Boyd's Marriage Index* (microfiche 94/2144), arranged by county with records of brides and grooms; *Boyd's Marriage Index, 1538–1837, Second Series* (microfiche 94/2143), and *Boyd's Marriage Index, 1538–1837, 3rd Series* (microfiche 94/2147), both arranged by bride and groom. The second and third series are sometimes referred to as the miscellaneous series. These indexes are useful in determining the date and place of a marriage as well as the particular parish in which it occurred. They may also help in estimating the frequency of a surname in a particular geographical area, or to identify the place of origin of someone who married in England before emigrating to North America or elsewhere.

The microfiche at the Library of Congress was reproduced from a copy at the Family History Library in Salt Lake City which, in turn, was made from the original *Boyd's Marriage Index* at the Society of Genealogists in London. Several editions of *A List of Parishes in Boyd's Marriage Index* have been published by the Society, so it is well to consult the Library of Congress computer catalog to determine the most recent one. The *Lists* also provide some detailed and useful information about the *Index*.

Local History

41.

Emmison, F. G. (Frederick George).

> Archives and local history / [by] F. G. Emmison.—2nd ed.—
> Chichester : Phillimore, 1974.—iii–xvi, 112 p., 32 p. of plates :
> ill., facsims., maps. **DA1 .E45 1974**
>> Bibliography: p. 105–106.

42.

Humphreys, Arthur Lee.

> A handbook to county bibliography : being a bibliography of bib-
> liographies relating to the counties and towns of Great Britain
> and Ireland / by Arthur L. Humphreys.—London : Printed by
> Strangeways and sons, 1917.—x, 501 p. **Z2023.A1 H9**
>> Reprinted in London by Dawsons in 1974.
>> **(Z2001.A1 H84 1974)**.

43.

Pugh, Ralph Bernard.

> The Victoria history of the counties of England; general intro-
> duction / edited by R. B. Pugh.—London : Published for the
> Institute of Historical Research by Oxford University Press,
> 1970.—xi, 282 p. **DA670.A1 P83**
>> Includes bibliographical references.
>> The Victoria histories of the counties of England represent
> scholarly local history research. Begun around 1900 this project
> has published local history volumes for some 30 percent of the
> English counties. Among the subjects included are the Domesday
> Books, bibliographies, eminent persons, maps, topographical
> accounts of parishes and manors, parish histories (including reli-
> gious houses), and descriptions of hospitals, industries, schools,
> and sports. For two counties, Northamptonshire and Hertford-
> shire, there are separate genealogy volumes.

> ————— ————— Supplement, 1970–90 / edited by C. R.
> Elrington.—ix, 80 p. **DA670.A1 V5 1990**

44.

Stephens, W. B.

> Sources for English local history / W. B. Stephens.—Rev. and
> expanded ed.—Cambridge ; New York : Cambridge University
> Press, c1981.—xv, 342 p.—(The Sources of history, studies in
> the uses of historical evidence). **Z2023 .S8 1981**
>> Reprinted 1994 by Phillimore & Co. **(Z2023.S8 1994)**
>> Includes bibliographical references and index.

45.
West, John.
　　Town records / John West.—Chichester, Sussex : Phillimore, 1983.—xviii, 366 p., [16] p. of plates. : ill.

DA690.A1 W47 1983
　　Includes bibliographical references and index.

46.
West, John.
　　Village records / with a foreword by W. G. Hoskins.—London : Macmillan ; New York : St. Martin's Press, 1962.—xvi, 208 p. : ill., maps, facsims.　　　**DA1 .W45 1962**
　　Includes bibliographical references.

Biographical Information ⤨

47.
Crockford's clerical directory.—Vol. 1 (1858)– .—London : Oxford University Press, [1858–　　　**BX5031.C8**

48.
Dictionary of national biography / edited by Leslie Stephen [and Sidney Lee]—London : Smith, Elder, 1885–1901.

DA28.D4
　　Contents: v. l–[63], Abbadie-Zuylstein.—Supplement v. l–3, Abbott-Woodward.
　　Founded in 1882, first published in 66 v.
　　Several supplements issued.
　　A collection of biographical sketches of noteworthy inhabitants of England from early times to the present.

——— 1961–1970 : with an index covering the years 1901–1970 in one alphabetical series / edited by E.T. Williams and C. S. Nicholls.—Oxford ; New York : Oxford University Press, 1981.—xviii, 1178 p.

——— 1971–1980 : with an index covering the years 1901–1980 in one alphabetical series / edited by Lord Blake and C. S. Nicholls.—Oxford ; New York : Oxford University Press, 1986.—xix, 1010 p.

——— 1981–1985 : with an index covering the years 1901–1985 : with an index covering the years 1901–1985 in one alphabetical series / edited by Lord Blake and C. S. Nicholls.—[Oxford] ; New York : Oxford University Press, 1990.—xiii, 518 p.

―――― 1986–1990: *With an index covering the years 1901–1990 in one alphabetical series.* edited by C. S. Nicholls; consultant editor, Sir Keith Thomas. Oxford; New York: Oxford University Press, 1996.—xiv, 607 p.

49.
Jacobs, Phyllis M.
Registers of the universities, colleges, and schools of Great Britain and Ireland / a list compiled by Phyllis M. Jacobs.— [London] : University of London, published for the Institute of Historical Research by the Athlone Press, 1964.—50 p.

Z5815.G5 J33

A guide to lists of students of English universities, colleges, and schools.

Heralds examining a seventeenth-century cartouche in the library of the College of Arms, London, England. LC–USZ62–113018, Lot 3556. Library of Congress, Prints and Photographs Division.

50.
Who was who : a companion to Who's who, containing the
biographies of those who died.—(Vol [1] 1897/1916)– .—
London : A. & C. Black, [1917?–   **DA28.W65**

――― : a cumulated index, 1897–1990.—New York : St.
Martin's Press, 1991.—vi, 801 p.   **DA28.W65 Suppl.**

Biographical Information on Microfilm

British Biographical Archive (microfiche 86/901) is a single-
alphabet cumulation of 324 of the most important English-
language biographical reference works published between 1601
and 1929. Included are some 240,000 persons of local, regional,
national, and international importance from England, Scotland,
Wales, and Ireland. The accompanying guide is the *British
Biographical Index* **(CT773.B75 1990 MicRR)**.

The British Biographical Archive. Series 2 (microfiche 97/1)
continues the numbering of the first series in a single-alphabet
cumulation of 268 source works originally published between
1601 and 1978. Included are some 170,000 persons, mainly
from the period 1870 to 1940.

British and Irish Biographies, 1840–1940 (microfiche
88/161) lists information from 273 biographical dictionaries
published between 1840 and 1940. Included are general biographical collections, as well as specialist, professional, and
regional biographical dictionaries. Part 1 indexes biographical
information for more than 180,000 prominent and not-so-
prominent British and Irish persons. Part 2 reproduces individual biographical dictionaries in their entirety. Additional information may be available in the MicRR guide 135 at the Library
of Congress. The materials described above may be examined
in the Microform Reading Room.

Records

51.

Bourne, Susan.

    Records of the Church of England : a practical guide for the family historian / Susan Bourne and Andrew H. Chicken.—Maidstone, Kent : Prospect Litho, 1988.—1 v. (unpaged).

        CS415.B68 1988

52.

Cole, Jean A., 1944–

    In and around record repositories in Great Britain and Ireland / Jean Cole and Rosemary Church.—3rd ed.—Ramsey, Huntingdon, Cambs. : Family Tree Magazine, 1992.—138 p.

        CD1040.C65 1992

53.

Colwell, Stella.

    Dictionary of genealogical sources in the Public Record Office / Stella Colwell.—London : Weidenfeld and Nicolson, 1992.—xvii, 206 p.   **Z5313.G69 C45 1992**

54.

Colwell, Stella.

    Family roots : discovering the past in the Public Record Office / Stella Colwell.—Rutland, Vt. : C. E. Tuttle Co., c1991.—231 p. : ill.   **CS415.C65 1991**

55.

Cox, Jane.

    Tracing your ancestors in the Public Record Office / by Jane Cox and Timothy Padfield.—4th ed. / by Amanda Bevan and Andrea Duncan.—London : H.M.S.O., 1990 (1991 printing)—266 p.—(Public Record Office handbooks ; no. 19).

        Z5313.G69 C69 1990

    Includes bibliographical references.

56.

Eakle, Arlene H.

    Descriptive inventory of the English collection / by Arlene H. Eakle, Arvilla Outsen, Richard S. Tompson.—Salt Lake City : University of Utah Press, 1979.—xvi, 168 p.—(Finding aids to the microfilmed manuscript collection of the Genealogical Society of Utah ; no. 3).   **Z5313.G69 E23**

57.

Foster, Janet.

British archives : a guide to archive resources in the United
Kingdom / Janet Foster & Julia Sheppard.—New York :
Stockton Press, 1989.—lviii, 834 p.   **CD1040 .F67 1989**
    Bibliography: p. liii–lviii.

58.

Gibson, Jeremy Sumner Wycherley.

Record offices : how to find them / Jeremy Gibson and Pamela
Peskett.—6th ed.—Birmingham, England : Federation of
Family History Societies, 1993.—60 p. : chiefly maps.
                                                  CD1040.G53 1993

59.

Grannum, Guy.

Tracing your West Indian ancestors : sources in the Public
Record Office / by Guy Grannum.—London : PRO
Publications, 1995.—x, 102 p. : facsims., 1 col. map.—(Public
Record Office reader's guide ; no. 11).   **CS203.G73 1995**

60.

Great Britain. Public Record Office.

Guide to the contents of the Public Record Office.—London :
H.M.S.O., 1963–1968.—3 v.   **CD1043 .A553**
    Contents: v. 1. Legal records, etc.—v. 2. State papers and
departmental records—v. 3. Documents transferred 1960–1966.

61.

Moulton, Joy Wade.

Genealogical resources in English repositories / by Joy Wade
Moulton.—Columbus, Ohio : Hampton House, 1988.—xxxiv,
614 p. : ill., maps.   **Z5313.G69 M94 1988**
    Includes bibliographical references and index.
    Supplement in pocket.

62.

The Nation's memory : a pictorial guide to the Public Record
Office / edited by Jane Cox, with contributions by David
Thomas, Timothy Padfield, and Michael Judd.—London :
H.M.S.O., 1988.—viii, 56 p. : ill. (some col.)
                                          CD1043.3.N38 1988

63.

Owen, Dolores B.

Guide to genealogical resources in the British Isles / by Dolores B.
Owen.—Metuchen, N. J. : Scarecrow Press, 1989.—x, 399 p. : ill.
                                      Z5305.G7 O94 1989

Effigies and heraldic banners in church at Compton Winyates, county Warwick, England. Illustrated in *Histories of Noble British Families with Bibliographical Notices of the Most Distinguished Individuals in Each* by Henry Drummond, London: William Pickering, 1846, CS419.D7 1846 folio, vol. 1, p. 35. Library of Congress.

64.

Record repositories in Great Britain : a geographical directory / the Royal Commission on Historical Manuscripts.—9th ed., 2nd impression (with revisions)—London : H.M.S.O., 1992.— vi, 46 p. **CD1040.R43 1992**

Includes bibliographical references (p. 42) and index.

65.

Reid, Judith P.

Genealogical research in England's Public Record Office : a guide for North Americans / Judith Prowse Reid.—Baltimore : Genealogical Pub. Co, 1996.—xiv, 148 p. : ill. **CS49.R45 1996**

"Local record offices of England and Wales": p. 85–93.

Includes bibliographical references (p. 115–135) and indexes.

66.

Rodger, N. A. M., 1949–

Naval records for genealogists / N. A. M. Rodger.—London : H.M.S.O., 1988.—iv, 220 p.—(Public Record Office handbooks ; no. 22). **Z5313.G69 R63 1988**

Bibliography: p. 200.

Historical Collections
on Microfilm ❧

The Foreign Copying Program was begun in 1905 to transcribe manuscripts relating to American history in the British Museum (now the British Library), the Bodleian Library in Oxford, and the Public Record Office (PRO). Many of these records are of interest to genealogists. For example, PRO records of individuals and families emigrating; original correspondence regarding America and the West Indies (Colonial Office 5); documents regarding American Loyalists (Audit Office 12 and 13); West New Jersey Society records, 1675–1921 (land records Treasury Solicitor 12); and army pensioners encouraged to emigrate to New South Wales and New Zealand from 1846 to 1851 (War Office 1). At the Library of Congress the guide, *Public Record Office Genealogy, a Selection of Leaflets,* and the compiler's *Genealogical Research in England's Public Record Office: a Guide for North Americans* (**CS49.R45 1996**) may be consulted in the Library of Congress Manuscript Division Reading Room.

While there is no complete list of the British manuscripts, those copied before 1944 are described by Grace Gardner Griffin in *A Guide to Manuscripts Relating to American History in British Depositories* (**CD1048.U5 A35 1946**). More recent acquisitions are listed in the 1976 imprint, *Manuscripts on Microfilm: A Checklist of the Holdings in the Manuscript Division* (**Z6621.U572 1975**). Visitors to the Library of Congress may consult these indexes in the Manuscript Reading Room. Most of the British manuscripts relating to American history on microfilm are available for use through interlibrary loan. Arrangements should be made through a local library.

The *British Manuscripts Project* (microfilm 041) includes manuscripts from the Cambridge University Library, the Public Record Office (including the Colonial Office), Lincoln Cathedral, Oxford University (Bodleian Library), the National Library of Wales, and several country house libraries (Longleat, Holkham Hall, Penshurst, Knole, Woburn Abbey, and Syon House). An index to the collection is Lester K. Born's *British Manuscripts Project, A Checklist of the Microfilms Prepared in England and Wales for the American Council of Learned Societies, 1941–1945* (**Z6620.G7 U5**). Visitors to the Library of Congress may examine the index and the collection in the Microform Reading Room.

The *National Inventory of Documentary Sources in the United Kingdom* (Microfiche 85/235) is a list of published and unpublished finding aids for archive and manuscript collections in the United Kingdom. It does not provide copies of the records themselves. The scope of this project includes county record offices (Berkshire, Gloucester, Bristol, Essex), university and public libraries (Bodleian), and special and private repositories (Guildhall Library, National Library of Wales). Readers in the Library of Congress may consult guide no. 101 in the Microform Reading Room.

Records of the States of the United States of America ("Early State Records") on microfilm 1550, include local, county, and city records, as well as newspapers for British colonial America. Legislative, statutory law, constitutional, administrative, executive, and court records are indexed. *A Guide to the Microfilm Collection of Early State Records* (**Z663.96.G8**) is on reference in the Microform Reading Room.

Maps, Atlases, Gazetteers

67.
Gardner, David E.
> A genealogical atlas of England and Wales / compiled from original maps by David E. Gardner, Derek Harland, Frank Smith.—Salt Lake City : Deseret Book Co., c1960.—1 atlas (vii, 88 p.) : maps.   **G1815.G3 1962 <G&M>**

68.
Hindle, Brian Paul.
> Maps for local history / Brian Paul Hindle.—London : B. T. Batsford, 1988.—160 p. : maps.—(Batsford local history series).   **DA1.H56 1988**

69.
Lewis, Samuel, d. 1865.
> A topographical dictionary of England, comprising the several counties, cities, boroughs, corporate and market towns, parishes, and townships, and the islands of Guernsey, Jersey, and Man, with historical and statistical descriptions : and embellished with engravings of the arms of the cities, bishoprics, universities, colleges, corporate towns, and boroughs ; and of the seals of the various municipal corporations / by Samuel Lewis—5th ed.—London : S. Lewis and Co., 1844.—4 v. ill. and atlas (1 leaf, 55 maps (part fold.) fold. plan).   **DA625.L676**

70.

Smith, Frank.

A genealogical gazetteer of England : an alphabetical dictionary of places, with their location, ecclesiastical jurisdiction, population, and the date of the earliest entry in the registers of every ancient parish in England.—Baltimore : Genealogical Pub. Co., 1968.—xv, 599 p. **DA640.S6**

Additional Geographical Resources

The Ordnance Survey Maps of Great Britain are county maps (six inches to the mile scale) which reflect the area in the mid to late nineteenth century, showing manor houses, castles, etc. Indexed by county, survey maps exist for England, Wales, and Scotland. There are also thousands of single-sheet maps of Great Britain, which may show estates, coats of arms, cities, and towns. Although there is no published list or catalog of these sheet maps, visitors to the Library of Congress Geography and Map Reading Room may request the help of a map librarian in locating the item desired.

Also available are historical indexes such as *Cassell's Gazetteer of Great Britain and Ireland* (**DA625.C344 1899**), *A Topographical Dictionary of Great Britain and Ireland, 1833* (**DA625.G675**), and *Gazetteer of the British Isles, 9th ed.* (**DA640.B23 1963**). In addition, hundreds of historical atlases of Great Britain, the earliest being the Saxton Atlas from the 1570s, can be examined in the Geography and Map Reading Room. More recent publications are the *Index of Place Names: Census 1961, England, Wales*, 1965 (**DA640.A25**) and *United Kingdom; Official Standard Names Approved by the United States Board on Geographic Names, 1950* (**DA640.U5**). Researchers in other libraries may consult a reference librarian for assistance.

Names, Geographical

71.
Cameron, Kenneth.
English place-names / Kenneth Cameron.—3rd ed.—London : B. T. Batsford, 1977, c1961.—258 p., [4] leaves of plates. : ill.

DA645.C3 1977

Bibliography: p. 229–233.

72.
Ekwall, Eilert, 1877–
The concise Oxford dictionary of English place-names.—4th ed.—Oxford : Clarendon Press, 1960.—546 p.

DA645 .E38 1960

Bibliography: p. xxxvi–xii.

73.
English Place-Name Society.
[Survey of English place-names].—Cambridge [Eng.] : The University press, 1924–   **DA645.A4**

Partial contents: vol. I. (Part 1) Introduction to the survey of English place-names; (Part 2) The chief elements used in English place-names, vol. II. The place-names of Buckinghamshire, vol. III. The place-names of Bedforshire and Huntingdonshire, vol. IV. The place-names of Worcestershire, vol. V. The place-names of the North Riding of Yorkshire, vols. VI, VII. The place-names of Sussex, Parts 1 and 2, vols. VIII, IX. The place-names of Devon, Parts 1 and 2, vol. X. The place-names of Northamptonshire, vol. XI. The place-names of Surrey, vol. XII. The place-names of Essex, vol. XIII. The place-names of Warwickshire, vol. XIV. The place-names of the East Riding of Yorkshire and York, vol. XV. The place-names of Hertfordshire, vol. XVI. The place-names of Wiltshire, vol. XVII. The place-names of Nottinghamshire, vol. XVIII. The place-names of Middlesex, vol. XIX. The place-names of Cambridgeshire and the Isle of Ely, vols. XX-XXII. The place-names of Cumberland, Parts 1, 2, and 3, vols. XXIII, XXIV. The place-names of Oxfordshire, Parts 1, and 2, vols. XXV, XXVI. English place-name elements, Parts 1 and 2, vols. XXVII–XXIX. The place-names of Derbyshire, Parts 1, 2, and 3, vols. XXX–XXXVII. The place-names of the West Riding of Yorkshire, Parts 1–8, vol. XXXVIII–XLI. The place-names of Gloucestershire, Parts 1–4, vol. XLII, XLIII. The place-names of Westmorland, Parts 1 and 2, vol. XLIV–XLVIII,LIV. The place-names of Cheshire, Parts 1–4, 5, I:i and ii, vols. XLIX–LI. The place-names of Berkshire, Parts 1, 2, and 3, vols. LII, LIII, LIX–LX. The place-names of Dorset, Parts 1–3, vol. LV. The place-names of Staffordshire, Part 1, vols. LVI, LVII. Cornish place-name elements, vols. LVIII, LXIV–LXVI, LXXI. The place-names of Lincolnshire, Parts 1–4, vol. LXI. The place-names of Norfolk, Part 1, vols, LXII–LXIII, LXX. The place-names of Shropshire, Parts 1 and 2, vol. LXVII–LXIX. The place-names of Rutland.

74.
Mills, A. D.
> A dictionary of English place names / A. D. Mills.—Oxford ; New York : Oxford University Press, 1993. **[DA645.M55 1993]**
> **Not yet in LC**

> ———— ———— 1991.—xxxi, 388 p. **DA645.M55 1991**

75.
Reaney, Percy H. (Percy Hide), 1880–1968.
> The origin of English place-names.—London : Routledge and Paul, [1960].—277 p. : ill. **DA645.R4**
> Bibliography: p. 243–246.
> Reprinted in London by Routledge and K. Paul in 1985.

Names, Personal ☜

76.
Bardsley, Charles Wareing Endell, 1843–1898.
> A dictionary of English and Welsh surnames : with special American instances / by the late Charles Wareing Bardsley ; revised for the press by his widow.—London ; New York : H. Frowde, 1901.—xvi, 837, [1] p. **CS2505.B3 1901**
> Reprinted in Baltimore by Genealogical Pub. Co. in 1967.

77.
Ewen, C. L'Estrange (Cecil L'Estrange), 1877–
> A history of surnames of the British Isles : a concise account of their origin, evolution, etymology, and legal status.—London, K. Paul, Trench, Trubner, Ltd., 1931.—xx, 508 p. **CS2505.E8**
> "A Short Bibliography": p. 429–436.
> Reprinted in Detroit by Gale Research Co. and in Baltimore by Genealogical Pub. Co. in 1968.

78.
Lasker, Gabriel Ward.
> Atlas of British surnames : with 154 maps of selected surnames / G. W. Lasker, C. G. N. Mascie-Taylor.—Detroit : Published for the Guild of One-Name Studies by Wayne State University Press, [1990].—x, 86 p. : maps. **CS2507.L37 1990**
> Includes bibliographical references (p. 7–8) and index.

79.

Reaney, Percy H. (Percy Hide), 1880–1968.
  A dictionary of British surnames / by P. H. Reaney.—3rd ed.
  with corrections and additions / by R. M. Wilson.—London ;
  New York : Routledge, 1991.—lxx, 508 p.   **CS2505.R39 1991**

80.

Reaney, Percy H. (Percy Hide), 1880–1968.
  The origin of English surnames / by P. H. Reaney.—New York :
  Barnes & Noble, [1967].—xix, 415 p.   **CS2505.R4**
    Bibliography: p. xvii–xix.

Domesday Book

The Domesday Book is the record of William the Conqueror's
survey of England in 1086. For the majority of English villages
and towns, the Domesday Book, organized by county, is the
starting point of their recorded history. This first English census, considered by some as the most remarkable administrative
accomplishment of the Middle Ages, provides a record of
English social organization in the Anglo-Norman period. As a
genealogical tool, however, its usefulness is limited. The works
listed below attempt to assist modern readers who want to consult the Book.

81.

Battle Abbey.
  The roll of Battle Abbey / annotated by John Bernard Burke.—
  [Reprinted in] Baltimore : Genealogical Pub. Co., 1978—107,
  p. : coats of arms.   **CS432.N7 B3 1978**
    Originally published in London by E. Churton in 1848.

82.

Domesday book / text and translation edited by John Morris.—
  Chichester : Phillimore, 1975–<1992 >.—<v. 1–38 in 39 >.—
  (History from the sources).   **DA190.D5 1975**
    English and Latin.
    Vols. 36–38 are Index. pt. 1: Places, pt. 2: Persons, and pt. 3:
  Subjects.

83.

The Domesday book : England's heritage, then and now /
editor, Thomas Hinde.—New York : Crown, 1985.—351 p. : ill.
(some col.), col. maps.   **DA190.D7 D66 1985**
    Bibliography: p. 343–346.

84.

Ellis, Henry, *Sir*, **1777–1869.**

A general introduction to Domesday book : accompanied by indexes of the tenants-in-chief, and under-tenants, at the time of the survey; as well as of the holders of lands mentioned in Domesday anterior to the formation of that record; with an abstract of the population of England at the close of the reign of William the Conqueror, so far as the same is actually entered / by Sir Henry Ellis.—[London : Printed by G. Eyre & A. Spottiswoode], 1833.—2 v.   **DA190.D7 E5**

Includes bibliographical references.

Reprinted in Baltimore by Genealogical Pub. Co. in 1971.

85.

The Norman people and their existing descendants in the British dominions and the United States of America—London : H. S. King & Co., 1874.—xvi, 484 p.   **CS432.N7 N7 1874**

"Alphabetical series of Norman names and families from the London post-office directory": p. 131–452.

Reprinted in Baltimore by Genealogical Pub. Co. in 1975.

Periodicals

86.

Family tree magazine.—v. 1, no. 2 (Jan.-Feb. 1985)- [Huntingdon, England : J. M. Armstrong], c1984–

CS410.F36

87.

The Genealogists' magazine : official organ of the Society of Genealogists.—Vol. 1 (Apr. 1925)– .—[London, 1925–

CS410.S61

88.

Harleian Society. London.

Publications.—Vol 1. (1869)– .—[London, 1869–   **CS410.H3**

Lists sixteenth- and seventeenth-century pedigrees and coats of arms recorded by College of Arms heralds.

City Directories

89.

Atkins, P. J. (Peter J.).
>The directories of London, 1677–1977 / P.J. Atkins.—London ;
>New York : Mansell, 1990.—732 p. : ill.   **Z5771.4.G7 A85 1990**
>>Includes bibliographical references and indexes.

90.

Goss, Charles William Frederick, 1864–
>The London directories, 1677–1855 : a bibliography with notes
>on their origin and development / by Charles W. F. Goss,
>F.S.A.—London : D. Archer, 1932.—xi, 146, p. : incl. front.
>(facsim.).   **Z5771.G67**

91.

Norton, Jane E. (Jane Elizabeth), 1893–
>Guide to the national and provincial directories of England and
>Wales, excluding London, published before 1856 / by Jane E.
>Norton.—London : Offices of the Royal Historical Society,
>1950.—vii, 241 p.—(Royal Historical Society [London],
>Guides and handbooks ; no. 5).   **Z5771.N6**
>>Reprinted with corrections in London by the Royal
>Historical Society in 1984.   **(Z2034.N67 1984)**

Religions

92.

Friends House Library digest registers of births, marriages, and
burials for England and Wales, 17th c.–1837 [microform].—
London : World Microfilms Publications, 1989.—32 microfilm
reels : maps.   **Microfilm 94/2114 (C) <MicRR>**
>GUIDE: Accompanied by printed guide entitled: *Quaker
>Digest Registers of Births, Marriages, and Burials for England and
>Wales, c. 1650–1837.* MicRR Guide No.: 329.
>>These original English and Welsh Quaker nonconformist
>records are now in the Public Record Office in London, as class
>RG6 General Register Office : Society of Friends' Registers and
>Certificates of Births, Marriages and Burials, 1613–1841.

93.

Huguenot Society of London.
>Publications.—Vol. 1 (1885/86)– .—Lymington, 1887–
>>   **BX9450.H8**
>>Vols. 1–23 available on microfilm (04095).

94.

Jackson, Ronald Vern.

Inventory of church records of the British Isles / editors, Ronald Vern Jackson, Gary Ronald Teeples, David Schaefermeyer.—Bountiful, Utah : Accelerated Indexing Systems, c1976.—109 p., [2] leaves of plates : maps.—(Encyclopedia of local history and genealogy ; ser. 2, v. 1). **CD1068.A2 J3**

95.

Lart, Charles Edmund.

Huguenot pedigrees.—London : The Saint Catherine Press, 1924–1928.—2 v. **CS432.H8 L3**

Vol. 2 published by C. Guimarsens [1928?].

Reprinted in Baltimore by Genealogical Pub. Co. in 1967. **(CS432.H8 L32).**

96.

Rosenstein, Neil.

The unbroken chain : biographical sketches and the genealogy of illustrious Jewish families from the 15th–20th century / Neil Rosenstein.—Rev. ed.—New York : CIS Publishers ; Elizabeth, N. J. : Computer Center for Jewish Genealogy, 1990.—2 v. (xix, 1323 p.) : ill. **CS31.R67 1990**

Includes bibliographical references and index.

Wills ~

97.

Camp, Anthony J.

Wills and their whereabouts / by Anthony J. Camp ; being a thorough revision and extension of the previous work of the same name by B. G. Bouwens.—[3rd rev., and enl. ed.].—Canterbury : Published for the Society of Genealogists by Phillimore, 1963.—xix, 137 p. **LAW <E Treatises>**

98.

Gibson, Jeremy Sumner Wycherley.

Probate jurisdictions : where to look for wills / compiled by Jeremy Gibson.—3rd ed.—Baltimore : Genealogical Pub. Co., 1989.—x, 62 p. : maps. **CD1066.A1 G53 1989**

99.

A List of wills, administrations, etc. in the Public Record Office, London, England, 12th–19th century.—Baltimore : Magna Carta Book Co., 1968.—ix, 158 p. **CS434 .L56**

100.

Pratt, David H.

Researching British probates, 1354–1858 : a guide to the microfilm collection of the Family History Library / David H. Pratt.—Wilmington, Del. : Scholarly Resources Inc., 1992– .—v <1 > : col. maps. **Z5313.G7 E57 1992**

Contents: v. 1. Northern England/Province of York—

Celtic no. 1, Celtic stone cross ornamentation; five designs found in churchyards throughout Scotland. LC–USZ62–112157, illustrated in *The Grammar of Ornament* by Owen Jones, London: Day and Son, Limited, 1965, NX1510.J7 1865, plate 63. Library of Congress, Prints and Photographs Division Case Y.

Chapter Two

Sources for Research in

cottish

Genealogy

CONTENTS

Handbooks

101.

Goldie, Douglas Bruce.

In search of Hamish McBagpipes : a concise guide to Scottish genealogy / Douglas Bruce Goldie.—Bowie, Md. : Heritage Books, 1992.—116 p.   **E184.S3 G65 1992**

Includes bibliographical references (p. [100]–111).

102.

Hamilton-Edwards, Gerald Kenneth Savery.

In search of Scottish ancestry / Gerald Hamilton-Edwards.—2nd ed.—Chichester, Sussex, England : Phillimore, 1983.—ix, 252 p. : ill.   **CS463.H35 1983**

Bibliography: p. 218–233.

102A.

Irvine, Sherry.

Your Scottish ancestry : a guide for North Americans / by Sherry Irvine.—Salt Lake City, Utah : Ancestry, c1997.—253 p. : ill., maps   **CS463.I78 1997**

103.

James, Alwyn.

Scottish roots: a step-by-step guide for ancestor-hunters / Alwyn James. Rev. ed.—Edinburgh : Saltire Society, 1995.

    CS464.J255 1995

104.

Johnson, Gordon.

Census records for Scottish families : a survey of census and related records useful in tracing Scottish fmilies at home and abroad / by Gordon Johnson.—Aberdeen : Association of Scottish Family History Societies, 1990.—69 p.

    CS464.J64 1990

105.

Moody, David.

Scottish family history / David Moody.—Baltimore : Genealogical Pub. Co., 1994.—219 p.   **CS463.M66 1994**

Includes bibliographical references (p. [179]–213) and index.

106.

Reakes, Janet.

How to trace your Scottish ancestors : an A-Z approach / Janet Reakes.—Sydney, NSW : Hale & Iremonger, c1988.—67 p., [4] p. of plates : ill., maps.   **CS463.R43 1988**

107.

Scotland : a genealogical research guide.—Salt Lake City, Utah : Genealogical Library of the Church of Jesus Christ of Latter-Day Saints, c1987.—vi, 61 p. : ill.—(Series A / the Genealogical Library of the Church of Jesus Christ of Latter-Day Saints ; no. 60).   **CS463.S46 1987**
    Bibliography: p. 50–52.

108.

Sinclair, Cecil.

Tracing your Scottish ancestors : a guide to ancestry research in the Scottish Record Office / Cecil Sinclair.—Edinburgh : H.M.S.O., 1990 (1991 printing).—x, 153 p. : ill.
        CS463.S56 1990

109.

Steel, D. J. (Donald John)

National index of parish registers. Edited by D. J. Steel and Mrs. A. E. F. Steel. London : Society of Genealogists 1966–<1996>.v. <1–5>, v.6, pts. 1–5; v.7; v.8, pts. 1–2; v.9, pts. 1–5; v. 10, pt. 1; v.11, pt. 1; v. 12; in 16>.   **CD1068.A2 S8**
    See Vol. 12 *Sources for Scottish Genealogy and Family History.*

Pedigrees and Family Histories

110.

Ferguson, Joan P. S.

Scottish family histories / compiled by Joan P S. Ferguson, assisted by Dennis Smith and Peter Wellburn.—Edinburgh : National Library of Scotland, 1986.—xii, 254 p.
        Z5313.S4 F39 1986

111.

Stuart, Margaret.

Scottish family history : a guide to works of reference on the history and genealogy of Scottish families / by Margaret Stuart ; to which is prefixed an essay on how to write the history of a family, by James Balfour Paul.—Edinburgh : Oliver and Boyd, 1930.—vii, 386 p., 3 leaves.   **Z5313.S4 S9**
    Bibliography: p. 385–386.
    Reprinted in Baltimore by Genealogical Pub. Co. in 1978.

Bibliographies

112.

Ferguson, Joan P. S.

Directory of Scottish newspapers / compiled by Joan P. S. Ferguson.—[2nd ed.].—Edinburgh : National Library of Scotland, 1984.—xviii, 155 p. : ill. **Z6956.G6 F47 1984**

Bibliography: p. xvii–xviii.

113.

Hancock, P. D.

A bibliography of works relating to Scotland, 1916–1950.—Edinburgh : University Press, [c1959–1960].—2 v.—(Edinburgh University publications). **Z2061.H3**

Intended as a supplement to *A Contribution to the Bibliography of Scottish Topography* by Sir Arthur Mitchell and C. G. Cash, published in 1917 by the Scottish History Society.

114.

Matheson, Cyril.

A catalogue of the publications of Scottish historical and kindred clubs and societies and of the papers relative to Scottish history issued by H.M. Stationery Office including the Reports of the Royal Commission on historical mss, 1908–1927 with a subject index by Cyril Matheson.—Aberdeen : Milne and Hutchison, 1928. viii, 232 p. **Z2061.T34**

Includes 1908 through 1927. For materials issued before 1908 see Terry's Catalogue (no. 119).

115.

Mitchell, Arthur, *Sir*, 1826–1909.

A contribution to the bibliography of Scottish topography / by the late Sir Arthur Mitchell, K. C. B., and C. G. Cash.—Edinburgh : Printed by T. and A. Constable for the Scottish History Society, 1917.—2 v.—(Publications of the Scottish History Society ; 2nd ser., v. 14–15).

DA750.S25 2d ser., vol. 14, 15

116.

National Library of Scotland.

Catalogue of manuscripts acquired since 1925.—Edinburgh : [H.M. Stationery Off.], 1938–<1989>.—v. <1–7>.

Z6621.N279 N37 1938

Contents: v. 1. Manuscripts 1–1800, charters and other formal documents 1–900—v. 2. Manuscripts 1801–4000, charters and other formal documents 901–2634—v. 3. Manuscripts 4001–4940: Blackwood papers, 1805–1900—v. 4. Manuscripts 4941–6405, charters and other formal documents 2635–6000—

v. 5. Manuscripts 6406–7529—v. 6. Manuscripts 7530–8022, Scottish foreign mission records, 1827–1929—v. 7. Manuscripts 8023–9500, charters and other formal documents 7637–8500.

117.
New York Public Library.
A list of works relating to Scotland / comp. by George F. Black, Ph.D.—[New York] : The New York Public Library, 1916.— viii, 1233 p.   **Z2069.N39**
"Reprinted, with additions . . . from the *Bulletin*, January-December, 1914."

118.
Stevenson, David, Ph.D.
Scottish texts and calendars : an analytical guide to serial publications / David and Wendy B. Stevenson.—London : Royal Historical Society ; Edinburgh : Scottish History Society, 1987.—xii, 233 p.—(Scottish History Society ; 4th ser., v. 23) (Guides and handbooks ; no. 14).   **DA750.S25 4th ser., vol. 23**
Companion vol. to: Mullins's *Texts and calendars,* 1958 (no. 33) and his *Texts and calendars II,* 1983 (no. 34).

119.
Terry, Charles Sanford, 1864–1936.
A catalogue of the publications of Scottish historical and kindred clubs and societies, and of the volumes relative to Scottish history issued by His Majesty's Stationery Office, 1780–1908 with a subject index by Charles Sanford Terry.—Aberdeen : Printed for the University, 1909.—xiii, 253 p.   **Z2061.T33**
For materials issued from 1908 to 1927, see Matheson's Catalogue (no. 114).

Parish and Other Registers

Parish registers are church records that document births, marriages, and deaths. Few Scottish parish registers have been published. Unpublished Scottish parish registers are at the New Register House, Princes Street, Edinburgh 1, Scotland. Microfilm copies of these records are available at the Family History Library, Salt Lake City, Utah.

120.

Bloxham, V. Ben.

> Key to the parochial registers of Scotland : from earliest times through 1854 / compiled by V. Ben Bloxham, in consulation with Derek F. Metcalfe.—2nd ed.—Provo, Utah : Stevenson's Genealogical Center, 1979, c1970.—vi, 212 p.
>
> **Z5313.G7 B57 1979**
>
> Based on the *Detailed list of the old parochial registers of Scotland*, 1872.

121.

Cowan, Ian Borthwick.

> The parishes of medieval Scotland / by Ian B. Cowan.— Edinburgh : Scottish Record Society, 1967.—xv, 226 p.— (Scottish Record Society. Publications ; v. 93). **CS460.S4 vol. 93**

122.

Escott, Anne.

> Census returns and old parochial registers on microfilm : a directory of public library holdings in the west of Scotland / compiled by Anne Escott ; with parish atlas by J. Scott Fairie.— Rev. ed.—[Glasgow] : Glasgow District Libraries, Publications Board, 1986.—64 p. : maps.   **Z5313.G7 S363 1986**

123.

Scotland. General Registry Office of Births, Deaths and Marriages.

> Detailed list of the old parochial registers of Scotland.—Edinburgh : printed by Murray and Gibb for the Registrar-General of Births, Deaths, and Marriages, 1872.—144 p. **CD1098.A2 A2**
>
> Also published in National Genealogical Society *Quarterly*.—Vol. 44–45 (1955–1956).
>
> Lists parish registers at New Register House, Edinburgh.

124.

Scotland. General Registry Office of Births, Deaths and Marriages.

> A guide to the public records of Scotland deposited in H.M. General Register House, Edinburgh / by M. Livingstone.— Edinburgh : H.M. General Register House, 1905.—xxvii, 233 p.   **CD1072.A3**
>
> Updated in *Scottish Historical Review*.—Vol. 26 (1946) and annually through 1975.

125.

Scotland. Record Office.

> Index to register of deeds preserved in H.M. General Register House.—Edinburgh : H.M. Stationery Off., 1915–
>
> **CD1076 1915**
>
> From 1915 to the present the Scottish Record Office has published two index series: deeds and sasines. For a list of indexes to these records in the Scottish Record Office, Historical Search Room, see *Scottish Record Office Leaflet No. 19.*

126.

Scottish Record Office.

Index to Secretary's and particular registers of sasines for sher-
iffdoms of Inverness, Ross, Cromarty and Sutherland preserved
in H.M. General Register House.—Edinburgh, : H.M.S.O.,
1966– .—v.<1, 2>.—(Its Indexes ; no. 61).   **D1076 1915 no. 61**

Contents: v. 1. 1606–1608, 1617–1660—v. 2. 1661–1721—
Sasines record seventeenth-century city or sheriffdom land
ownership.

Local History ☙

127.

Armstrong, Norma E. S.

Local collections in Scotland / by Norma E. S. Armstrong.—
Glasgow : Scottish Library Association, 1977.—ix, 173 p.—
(Scottish library studies ; no. 5).   **Z2063.A1 A76**

Bibliography: p. 168.
Originally presented as the author's thesis, University of
Strathclyde, 1976.

128.

Moody, David.

Scottish local history : an introductory guide / David Moody.—
London : B. T. Batsford, 1986.—178 p., [8] p. of plates : ill.—
(Batsford local history series).   **DA759.M66 1986**

Bibliography: p. [170]–171.
Reprinted in Baltimore by Genealogical Pub. Co. in 1990.

129.

Sinclair, John, *Sir,* **1754–1835.**

The statistical account of Scotland, 1791–1799 / edited by Sir
John Sinclair.—[New ed. / general editors, Donald J.
Withrington and Ian R. Grant].—East Ardsley, Eng. : E. P.
Publishing, <1977–1983 >.—v. <1, 3, 5–6, 8, 10, 12, 14–18 >.

                    DA855.S5 1977

Includes bibliographical references and indexes.
Reprint of the 1791–1799 ed. published by Creech,
Edinburgh; with new arrangement and new introductions.

Biographical Information

130.

Anderson, William, 1805–1866.

The Scottish nation; or The surnames, families, literature, honours, and biographical history of the history of the people of Scotland.—Edinburgh: A. Fullarton & Co. [1859]–63.—3 v. in 9. fronts., ill., ports., coats of arms.   **CT813.A6**

Facsimile edition published in Bowie, Maryland, by Heritage Books in 1995.

131.

Chambers, Robert, 1802–1871.

A biographical dictionary of eminent Scotsmen.—New ed., rev. throughout and continued by Thomas Thomson.—London : Blackie and son, 1870.—3 v. : ill., ports.   **CT813.C5 1870**

Facsimile edition published in New York by G. Olms in 1971.

132.

Chambers Scottish biographical dictionary / editor, Rosemary Goring.—Edinburgh ; New York : Chambers, 1992.—xl, 468 p.   **DA758.C48 1992**

133.

Donaldson, Gordon.

Who's who in Scottish history / [by] Gordon Donaldson and Robert S. Morpeth.—New York : Barnes & Noble Books, [1973].—xx, 254 p. : ill.   **DA758.D66 1973b**

Includes bibliographical references.

134.

Foster, Joseph, 1844–1905.

Members of Parliament, Scotland, including the minor barons, the commissioners for the shires, and the commissioners for the burghs, 1357–1882, on the basis of the parliamentary return 1880 with genealogical and biographical notices / by Joseph Foster.—2nd ed. Rev. and cor.—London and Aylesbury : Priv. print. by Hazell, Watson and Viney, 1882.—xviii, 360 p.

Microfilm (61520 JN) <MicRR>

135.

MacDougall, Donald, 1854–1920.

Scots and Scots' descendants in America / D. MacDougall, editor in chief.—New York : Caledonian Pub. Co., [c1917].—v. 1 : ill. (incl. ports.).   **E184.S3 M14**

Only one volume published.

Bibliography: v. 1, p. 133–139.

136.

Reeks, Lindsay S.

Scottish coalmining ancestors / by Lindsay S. Reeks.—Baltimore : Gateway Press, 1986.—292 p. : ill. **CS476.C6 R44 1986**
Bibliography : p. 263–271.

137.

Taylor, James, 1813–1892.

The great historic families of Scotland / by James Taylor.—London : J. S. Virtue & Co., 1887.—2 v.
Microfilm (19659 DA) <MicRR>
Reprinted in Baltimore by Genealogical Pub. Co. in 1995
(DA758.3.A1T2 1995).

138.

Watt, Donald Elmslie Robertson.

A biographical dictionary of Scottish graduates to A.D. 1410 / by D. E. R. Watt.—Oxford : Clarendon Press, 1977.—xlii, 607 p. **CT813.W37 1977**
Revision and expansion of the author's thesis, Oxford University.

Maps, Atlases, Gazetteers

139.

Bartholomew, John.

Philip's handy atlas of the counties of Scotland.—New and rev. ed.—London : G. Philip & Son, 1898.—3 p. leaves, 34 p., 32 maps. **G1825.B3 1898 (G&M)**

140.

Gardner, David E.

A genealogical atlas of Scotland / compiled from original maps by David E. Gardner, Derek Harland [and] Frank Smith.—Salt Lake City : Bookcraft, [1962].—32 p. of maps, 34 p.
G1826.E1 G3 1962 (G&M)

141.

Groome, Francis H. (Francis Hindes), 1851–1902.

Ordnance gazetteer of Scotland : a graphic and accurate description of every place in Scotland / ed. by Francis H. Groome.—New ed. with census appendix.—Edinburgh : T. C. and E. C. Jack, 1901.—2 p. leaves, 1762 p. : ill., fold. map.
DA865.G87

In double columns, this edition contains all the printed matter of the large six-volume edition, the revisions made in 1895, and subsequent partial revisions.

142.

An Historical atlas of Scotland, c400–c1600 / edited by Peter McNeill and Ranald Nicholson ; cartographer J. W. Davie.— St. Andrews : Atlas Committee of the Conference of Scottish Medievalists, 1975.—x, 213 p. : maps (1 col.).

G1826.S1 H5 1975

Includes bibliographies.

143.

Lewis, Samuel, d. 1865.

A topographical dictionary of Scotland. Comprising the several counties, islands, cities, burgh and market towns, parishes, and principal villages, with historical and statistical descriptions: embellished with a large map of Scotland, and engravings of the seals and arms of the different burghs and universities.—London : S. Lewis and Co., 1846.—2 v. and atlas : ill. **DA865.L67**

The atlas consists of a sectional map of Scotland, scale five miles to the inch, in six folded sheets, with a view of Melrose Abbey (sheet 5).

Reprinted in Baltimore by Genealogical Pub. Co. in 1989.

144.

Moncreiffe of that Ilk, Iain, *Sir*, 1919–

Scotland of old : ancient territories of Scottish clans or considerable families, with arms of their chiefs or heads / approved by the Standing Council of Scottish Chiefs and by the Lord Lyon King of Arms.—— Edinburgh : Bartholomew, c1983.—1 map : col. ; 94 x 71 cm. **G5771.E6225 1983.M6**

Reprinted by Bartholomew in 1991 and 1994.

Copyright "By Sir Iain Moncreiffe of that Ilk, Bart., Ph.D., Albany Herald, and Don Pottinger, M.A., D.A., Unicorn Pursuivant of Arms."

Includes text and colored illustration of "The arms of the realm and ancient local principalities of Scotland," and indexed colored illustrations of clan arms.

145.

Smith, Frank, 1917–

A genealogical gazetteer of Scotland : an alphabetical dictionary of places . . . / compiled by Frank Smith.—Logan, Utah : Everton Publishers, [1979].—xxiii, 140 p. : maps. **DA869.S56**

DZ

Eighteenth-century Scottish costumes, including tartans. Illustrated in *Le Costume Historique* by Albert Charles Auguste Racinet, Paris: Firmin-Didot et cie, 1876, GT513.R2 1876, vol. VI, plate DZ. Library of Congress.

Names,
Geographical

146.

Darton, Michael.

The dictionary of Scottish place names : and the elements that
go to make them up / Mike Darton.—Moffat : Lochar, 1990.—
282 p.   DA869.D37 1990

147.

Great Britain. General Register Office (Scotland).

Index of Scottish place names from 1971 census, with location
and population over 100 persons / General Register Office,
Scotland.—Edinburgh : H.M.S.O., 1975.—xi, 186 p. : map.
                                                      HB2047.S33 1975

148.

Johnston, James Brown, 1862–

Place-names of Scotland / by James B. Johnston.—3rd ed.
reprinted, with additional notes on the author.—Wakefield : S.
R. Publishers, 1970.—xvi, 335 p.   DA869.J72 1970
  Bibliography: p. 327.
  A facsimile reprint of the 3rd ed. was published in London
by J. Murray in 1934.

149.

Mackenzie, W. C. (William Cook), 1862–1952.

Scottish place-names / by W. C. Mackenzie.—London, K. Paul,
Trench, Trübner & Co., 1931.—xi, 319, [1] p.   DA869.M14

150.

Nicolaisen, W. F. H.

Scottish place-names : their study and significance / [by]
W. F. H. Nicolaisen.—London : Batsford, 1976.—xxviii, 210 p.
: maps.   DA869.N53
  Bibliography: p. [xiv]–xxi.

151.

Watson, William J. (William John), 1865–1948.

The history of the Celtic place-names of Scotland / being the
Rhind lectures on archaeology (expanded) delivered in 1916, by
William J. Watson. Published under the auspices of the Royal
Celtic Society.—Edinburgh and London : W. Blackwood &
Sons, Ltd., 1926.—3 p. leaves, ix–xx, 558 p.   DA869.W3
  Reprinted in Shannon by Irish University Press in 1973.

Names, Personal

152.
Black, George Fraser, 1866–

The surnames of Scotland : their origin, meaning, and history / by George F. Black, Ph.D.—New York : The New York Public Library, 1946.—lxxi, [1], 838 p. : front. (port.).   **CS2435.B55**

"List of the Principal Works Referred to" : p. 835–838.

"Glossary of Obsolete or Uncommon Scots Words" : p. lix–lxxi.

Reprinted from the *Bulletin* of the New York Public Library.—(Aug. 1943–Sept. 1946).

153.
Dorward, David Philip.

Scottish surnames / [by] David Dorward ; illustrated by John Mackay.—Edinburgh : Blackwood, 1978.—ix, 70 p. : ill.— (Scottish connection).   **CS2435.D67**

154.
Dunkling, Leslie, 1935–

Scottish Christian names : an A-Z of first names / [by] Leslie Alan Dunkling.—London : Johnston and Bacon, 1978.—vii, 151 p.   **CS2375.S35 D66**

Bibliography: p. [139]–141.

155.
Sims, Clifford Stanley, 1839–1896.

The origin and signification of Scottish surnames. With a vocabulary of Christian names.—Albany, N.Y. : J. Munsell, 1862.—122 p.   **CS2435.S5**

Bibliographical references included in "Introduction" (p. [3]–7).

Reprinted in Rutland, Vt. by C. E. Tuttle Co. in 1969.

Periodicals

156.
The Highlander.—Began in 1963.—[Barrington, Ill. : A. J. Ray], 1963–   **E184.S3 H5**

Currently published seven times a year.

Includes annual directory issue, <1983– >.

157.
Publications of the Scottish History Society.—Vol. 1–61 ; new ser., v. 1–20 ; 3rd ser., v. 1–55.—Edinburgh : Printed by T. and A. Constable for the Society, 1887–1964.   **DA750.S25**
    136 v. : ill., ports., maps (part fold.) facsims., plans.
    Contains the Society's report of the annual meeting, 1st– ; 1887–1919.

158.
Scottish antiquary, or, Northern notes and queries.—Vol. 1 (1886)–v. 17 (1903) ; 17 vol. in 10.—Edinburgh : 1886–1903.
                              DA750.S2
    Title varies.

159.
The Scottish genealogist.—v. 1 (Jan. 1954)– .—[Edinburgh] : Scottish Genealogy Society.   **CS460.S35**

160.
Scottish notes and queries.—Vol. 1, no. 1 (June 1887)–1935.— [Aberdeen : D. Wyllie and Son], 1888–1935.
                      Microfilm 86/8820 <MicRR>
    Microfilm. Washington, D.C. : Library of Congress Photoduplication Service, 1986. 4 microfilm reels.
    33 v. published in 3 series: v. 1–12, 1887–1899; ser. 2, v. 1–8,1899–1907; ser. 3, v. 1–13, 1923–1935. General index to ser. 1, 1887–1899 in v. 12, 1901.

161.
Scottish Record Society.
    Publications.—Part I (Mar. 1898)– .—Edinburgh : Printed for the Society by James Skinner & Company, 1898–   **CS460.S4**
    Contains indexes and calendars, parish and other registers.

Directories

162.
The County directory of Scotland / postally ed. by George Massie ; comp. by Arthur Giles.—Edinburgh : A. Giles, [1912].—vii, [2], viii–xxv, 1169 p.   **DA866.C85 1912**
    Accompanied by Map of Scotland, reduced from the Ordnance survey by John Bartholomew (Edinburgh, A. Giles, [1912]). Scale ten miles to the inch.

163.

The County directory of Scotland (for 1901–1904) / postally ed. by George Massie ; compiled by Arthur Giles, proprietor and general editor—Edinburgh : R. Grant & Son, 1902.—xxxi, 1056 p. : ill., ports.   **DA866.C851**

164.

Findlay, James.

Directory to gentlemen's seats, villages, &c in Scotland : giving the counties in which they are situated—the post-towns to which each is attached—and the name of the resident . . . With a new map of Scotland, engr.. . . by Lizars ; collected and arr. by James Findlay.—Edinburgh : W.P. Kennedy, [1843].—4 p. leaves., 350, [1] p. : ill. front. (fold. map).   **DA865.F49**

165.

Scotland. Comptroller-General of Internal Revenue.

Owners of lands and heritages, 17 & 18 Vict., cap. 91. 1872–73. Return: I. Of the name and address of every owner of one acre and upwards in extent, outside the municipal boundaries of boroughs containing more than 20,000 inhabitants, with the estimated acreage, and the annual value of the lands and heritages of individual owners; and of the number of owners of less than one acre, with the estimated aggregate acreage and annual value of the lands and heritages of such owners in each county. II. A similar return for municipal boroughs containing more than 20,000 inhabitants.—Edinburgh : printed by Murray and Gibb, printers to H. M. Stationery Off., 1874.—iv, 211 p.   **LAW**

166.

Shaw, Gareth.

British directories : a bibliography and guide to directories published in England and Wales (1850–1950) and Scotland (1773–1950) / Gareth Shaw and Allison Tipper.—London ; New York : Leicester University Press, 1988, c1989.—440 p. : ill.   **Z5771.S45 1989**

Includes bibliographical references.

167.

Timperley, Loretta R.

A directory of landownership in Scotland, c1770 / edited by Loretta R. Timperley.—Edinburgh : Scottish Record Society, 1976.—x, 428 p. ([Publications] : New series—Scottish Record Society ; 5).   **HD614.T55**

Includes bibliographical references and index.

Religions

168.

Dictionary of Scottish church history & theology / organizing editor, Nigel M. de S. Cameron ; general editors, David F. Wright, David C. Lachman, Donald E. Meek.—Downers Grove, Ill. : InterVarsity Press, 1993.—xx, 906 p.

BR782.D43 1993

Includes bibliographical references.

169.

Free Church of Scotland.

Annals of the Free Church of Scotland, 1843–1900 / edited by the Rev. William Ewing.—Edinburgh : T. & T. Clark, 1914.—2 v.

BX9084.A4

"Ordained Ministers and Missionaries of the Free Church of Scotland, 1843–1900": vol. 1, p. 76–363.

170.

Scott, David, 1834–1897.

Annals and statistics of the original Secession Church till its disruption and union with the Free Church of Scotland in 1852 / chiefly compiled from official records by the Rev. David Scott.—Edinburgh : A. Elliot.—xv p., 1 leaf, 612 p. : ill., plates, ports., 2 facsim. (incl. fold. front), diagr.   **BX9083.S4**

171.

Scott, Hew, 1791–1872.

Fasti ecclesiae scoticanae : the succession of ministers in the Church of Scotland from the Reformation / by Hew Scott, D.D.—New ed., rev. and continued to the present time under the superintendence of a committee appointed by the General Assembly.—Edinburgh : Oliver and Boyd, 1915–<81 >.—v. <1–8, 10 > : front. (port.).   **BX9099.S4 1915**

Vols. 1–6 include "Bibliography of church and parish histories, etc."

Vol. 10 edited by Donald Farquhar Macleod Macdonald; published by Saint Andrew Press.

172.

United Free Church of Scotland.

Fasti, 1900–1929 / edited by John Alexander Lamb.—Edinburgh : Oliver and Boyd, [1956].—xi, 639 p. **BX9089.A53**

Clans and Tartans

173.

Adam, Frank.

> The clans, septs & regiments of the Scottish Highlands / rev. by Sir Thomas Innes of Learney.—8th ed.—Baltimore : Genealogical Pub. Co., 1970.—xii, 624 p. : ill. (part col.), coats of arms, ports.   **DA880.H6 A6 1970**
>> Includes bibliographical references.

174.

Bain, Robert.

> The clans and tartans of Scotland / [by] Robert Bain.—5th ed. / enlarged and re-edited by Margaret O. MacDougall ; heraldic adviser P.E. Stewart-Blacker ; with a foreword by the Countess of Erroll.—Glasgow : Collins, 1976.—320 p. : col. ill., coats of arms, col. maps (on lining papers).   **DA880.H76 B3 1976**
>> Bibliography: p. 318–319.

175.

Dunbar, John Telfer, 1912–

> The official tartan map of tartans approved by clan chiefs, the Standing Council of Scottish Chiefs, or the Lord Lyon King of Arms / by John Telfer Dunbar . . . and Don Pottinger.—London : Elm Tree Books, c1976.—col. map on sheet 122 x 90 cm.
>   **G5771.E6 1976 .D8**
>> Relief shown by shading.
>> "Map [copyright] John Bartholomew & Son Ltd. 1976."
>> Includes text, index to tartans, and col. illus. of 141 tartans.

176.

Eyre-Todd, George, 1862–

> The Highland clans of Scotland : their history and traditions / by George Eyre-Todd ; with an introduction by A. M. Mackintosh, with one hundred and twenty-two illustrations including reproductions of M'Ian's celebrated paintings of the costumes of the clan.—London : Heath, Cranton, 1923.—2 v. : ill., col. fronts., plates (some col.), ports.   **DA880.H6 E8**

177.

Grant, James, 1822–1887.

> The tartans of the clans of Scotland / also an introductory account of Celtic Scotland, clanship, chiefs, their dress, arms, emblazoned arms of the chiefs, and a map of the districts occupied by the various clans are added.—Edinburgh and London : W. & A. K. Johnston, 1886.—82 leaves : col. front. (port.), col. ill., 72 col. pl., map.   **DA880.H76 G7**

Each plate is accompanied by a leaf with descriptive letter-press and coat of arms in color.

Reprinted in New York by Dover Publications Inc. in 1992.

178.
Griest, Terry L.
Scottish tartans and family names / by Terry L. Griest.—
Annapolis, Md. : Harp & Lion Press, c1986.—vii, 133 p. : ill.
DA880.H76 G74 1986

179.
Grimble, Ian.
Scottish clans & tartans.—New York : Tudor Pub. Co.,
[1973].—272 p. : col. ill. **DA880.H6 G74**

Scottish tartans worn by children dancing in Scotland, 1900–1920. LC–USZ62–112123, Carpenter Collection, Lot 11475.Library of Congress, Prints and Photographs Division.

180.
Innes of Learney, Thomas, *Sir*, 1893–1971.
      The tartans of the clans and families of Scotland.—8th ed.—
      Edinburgh : Johnston and Bacon, 1971.—iv, 300 p., 2 plates :
      ill. (chiefly col.), coats of arms, ports.   **DA880.H76 I5 1971**

181.
Logan, James, 1794?–1872.
      The clans of the Scottish Highlands : the costumes of the clans
      / R.R. McIan ; text by James Logan ; foreword by Antonia
      Fraser.—1st American ed.—New York : Knopf, 1980.—206 p. :
      col. ill., map (on lining papers).   **DA880.H76 L7 1980**
      Originally published in 1845–47 by Ackermann, London.

182.
MacLean, Charles, 1951–
      The clan almanac : an account of the origins of the principal
      tribes of Scotland, illustrated with examples of the tartans
      adopted by each / Charles MacLean.—Moffat, Scotland :
      Lochar Pub., c1990.—144 p. : col. ill. **DA880.H76 M35 1990**
      Includes bibliographical references (p. 144).

183.
Martine, Roderick.
      Scottish clan and family names : their arms, origins, and tartans /
      Roddy Martine ; foreword by Sir Malcolm Innes of Edingight ;
      heraldic illustrations by Don Pottinger.—New rev. ed., new ed.—
      Edinburgh : Mainstream Pub., 1992.—224 p. : ill. (some col.),
      maps.   **DA880.H76 M37 1992**

184.
Scarlett, James Desmond.
      Tartan : the Highland textile / James D. Scarlett.—London :
      Shepheard-Walwyn, 1990.—xii, 204 p. : ill. (some col.).
                    DA880.H76 S36 1990

185.
Smith, Philip D., 1933–
      Tartan for me : suggested tartans for Scottish, Scotch-Irish,
      Irish, and North American surnames with lists of clan, family,
      and district tartans / by Philip D. Smith.—Expanded 6th ed.—
      Bowie, Md. : Heritage Books, 1994.—123 p. : maps.
                    DA880.H76 S55 1994

186.
Stewart, Donald C. (Donald Calder), 1893–
      The setts of the Scottish tartans : with descriptive and historical
      notes / by Donald C. Stewart.—2nd revised ed.—London :
      Shepheard-Walwyn (Publishers) Ltd., 1974.—xiii, 154 p., [1],
      viii leaves of plates : ill. (chiefly col.), coat of arms.
                    DA880.H76 S67 1974

      Bibliography: p. 113–117.

Emigration

187.

Adams, Ian.

Cargoes of despair and hope : Scottish emigration to North
America, 1603–1803 / Ian Adams and Meredyth Somerville.—
Edinburgh : J. Donald Publishers, c1993.—258 p. : ill., maps.

E49.2.S3 A33 1993

188.

Bumsted, J. M.

The people's clearance : Highland emigration to British
North America, 1770–1815 / J. M. Bumsted.—Edinburgh :
Edinburgh University Press ; Winnipeg, Canada : University of
Manitoba Press, c1982.—xvii, 305 p. : ill.   **F1035.S4 B85 1982**
Bibliography: p. [288]–295.

189.

Cameron, Viola Root.

Emigrants from Scotland to America, 1774–1775. Copied from
a loose bundle of Treasury papers in the Public Record Office,
England.—Baltimore : Southern Book Co., 1959.—117 p.

E187.5.C18 1959

190.

Dickson, R. J.

Ulster emigration to colonial America, 1718–1775 / by R. J.
Dickson.—London : Routledge & Kegan Paul, 1966.—xiv, 320
p. : map, tables.   **E184.S4 D47**
Reprinted in Belfast by the Ulster Historical Foundation in
1988.

191.

A Dictionary of Scottish emigrants into England & Wales /
complied by members of the Anglo-Scottish Family History
Society ; edited by J. D. Beckett—Manchester : The Society,
c1984–<c1992>. v. <1-5> : map.   **CS432.S3 D53 1984**

192.

Dobson, David.

Directory of Scots banished to the American plantations,
1650–1775 / by David Dobson.—Baltimore : Genealogical Pub.
Co., 1983.—vii, 239 p. : ill.   **E184.S3 D6 1983**

193.
Dobson, David.
Directory of Scottish settlers in North America, 1625–1825 /
by David Dobson.—Baltimore : Genealogical Pub. Co.,
1984–<1997 >.—v. <1–7 > : ill.   **E184.S3 D63 1984**

194.
Dobson, David.
The original Scots colonists of early America, 1612–1783 / by
David Dobson.—Baltimore : Genealogical Pub. Co., c1989.—
xi, 370 p.   **E49.2.S3 D63 1989**
Bibliography: p. viii–xi.

195.
Dobson, David.
Scottish emigration to Colonial America, 1607–1785 / David
Dobson.—Athens : University of Georgia Press, c1994.—266 p.
          E184.S3 D66 1994
Includes bibliographical references (p. [225]–241) and index.

196.
Donaldson, Gordon.
The Scots overseas.—London : Hale, 1966.—232 p. : [ill.],
plates, ports.   **DA774.5.D6 1966**
Reprinted in Westport, Conn. by Greenwood Press in 1976.

197.
Graham, Ian Charles Cargill, 1919–
Colonists from Scotland : emigration to North America,
1707–1783.—Ithaca, N.Y. : published for the American
Historical Association [by] Cornell University Press, [1956].—
x, 213 p. : map.   **E184.S3 G7**
Reprinted in Port Washington, N.Y. by Kennikat Press in
1972.

198.
Harper, Marjory.
Emigration from north-east Scotland / Marjory Harper.—
[Aberdeen] : Aberdeen University Press, <1988– >.—v. <1–2 > :
ill., maps, ports.   **JV7701.H37 1988**
Contents: v. 1. Willing exiles—v. 2. Beyond the Broad
Atlantic—
Bibliography: v. 1, p. 350–362.

199.
Hill, Douglas Arthur, 1935–
The Scots to Canada / by Douglas Hill.—London : Gentry
Books, 1972.—vii, 136 p. : ill. maps.   **JV7285.S35 H5**
200.

Insh, George Pratt.

Scottish colonial schemes, 1620–1686.—Glasgow : Maclehose, Jackson & Co., 1922.—6 p. leaves, 283 p. plates, 2 ports. (incl. front)., facsim.   **E188.I6**

201.

Perceval-Maxwell, M.

The Scottish migration to Ulster in the reign of James I / [by] M. Perceval-Maxwell.—London : Routledge & Kegan Paul ; New York : Humanities Press, 1973.—xx, 411 p. : ill.

DA990.U46 P47

202.

Steuart, Archibald Francis.

Papers relating to the Scots in Poland, 1576–1793 / ed. with an introduction by A. Francis Steuart.—Edinburgh : printed by T. and A. Constable for the Scottish History Society, 1915.— xxxix, 362 p.   **DA750.S25 vol. 59**

Also issued as *Publications* of the Scottish History Society, vol. 59.

A collection made by and in part edited by Beatrice Baskerville. Translations from Latin by J. Mackay Thomson.

203.

Whyte, Donald.

A dictionary of Scottish emigrants to Canada before confederation.—Toronto : Ontario Genealogical Society, 1968.—xvi, 443 p.

CS83.W48 1986

Bibliography: p. 439–443.

204.

Whyte, Donald.

A dictionary of Scottish emigrants to the U.S.A.—Baltimore : Magna Carta Book Co., 1972–1986.—2 v.   **E184.S3 W49**

Includes bibliographies and indexes.

"Volume 2: with an appendix of additions and corrections to volume 1."

Scottish Americans

205.
Aspinwall, Bernard, 1938–
> Portable utopia : Glasgow and the United States, 1820–1920 : with a comprehensive biographical list of the Scots and Americans who created the connection / Bernard Aspinwall.— [Aberdeen] : Aberdeen University Press, 1984.—xviii, 363 p., [4] p. of plates : ill.   **E184.S3 A86 1984**
>> Bibliography: p. 265–363.

206.
Black, George Fraser, 1866–1948.
> Scotland's mark on America / with a foreword by John Foord. New York : Scottish Section of "America's Making," 1921.— [San Francisco : R and E Research Associates, 1972].—126 p.   **E184.S3 B6 1972**
>> Bibliography: p. 117.

207.
Dobson, David.
> Directory of Scots in the Carolinas, 1680–1830 / by David Dobson.—Baltimore : Genealogical Pub. Co., 1986.—xi, 322 p. : ill.   **F265.S3 D63 1986**

208.
Dobson, David.
> Scots on the Chesapeake, 1607–1830 / compiled by David Dobson.—Baltimore : Genealogical Pub. Co., c1992.—xv, 169 p.   **F187.C5 D63 1992**

209.
Dobson, David.
> Scottish–American court records, 1733–1783 / David Dobson.—Baltimore : Genealogical Pub. Co., c1991.—105 p.   **E184.S3 D635 1991**

210.
Dobson, David.
> Scottish-American heirs, 1683–1883 / David Dobson.— Baltimore : Genealogical Pub. Co., c1990.—165 p.   **E184.S3 D637 1990**

211.
Dobson, David.
> Scottish-American wills, 1650–1900 / David Dobson.— Baltimore : Genealogical Pub. Co., c1991.   **E184.S3 D64 1991**

212.

Dunaway, Wayland Fuller, 1875–
> The Scotch-Irish of colonial Pennsylvania.—Chapel Hill :
> University of North Carolina Press, 1944.—vi p., 2 leaves,
> 3–273 p.   **F160.S4 D8**
>> Bibliography: p. 233–257.
>> Reprinted in Baltimore by Genealogical Pub. Co. in 1979.

213.

Hanna, Charles A[ugustus], 1863–
> The Scotch-Irish.—New York and London : G.P. Putnam's
> sons, 1902.—2 v. : front, maps.   **Microfilm 53597 E <MicRR>**
>> Reprinted in Baltimore by Genealogical Pub. Co. in 1968.

214.

Haws, Charles H.
> Scots in the Old Dominion, 1685–1800 / Charles H. Haws.—
> Edinburgh : J. Dunlop, c1980.—vii, 172 p. : maps.
>>   **E184.S3 H38 1980**

215.

Karras, Alan L.
> Sojourners in the sun : Scottish migrants in Jamaica and the
> Chesapeake, 1740–1800 / Alan L. Karras.—Ithaca : Cornell
> University Press, 1992.—xiii, 231 p. : ill., maps.
>>   **F187.C5 K37 1992**
>> Includes bibliographical references (p. [217]–226) and index.

216.

Landsman, Ned C., 1951–
> Scotland and its first American colony, 1683–1765 / Ned C.
> Landsman.—Princeton, N.J. : Princeton University Press,
> c1985.—xiv, 360 p. : maps.   **F145.S3 L36 1985**
>> Bibliography: p. 341–346.

217.

Lehmann, William Christian, 1888–
> Scottish and Scotch-Irish contributions to early American life
> and culture / William C. Lehmann.—2nd ed.—Washington :
> Lehmann-Spohr, 1980.—232 p.   **E183.8.G7 L36 1980**
>> Bibliography: p. 223–226.

218.

Le Roy, Bruce.
> Lairds, bard, and mariners : the Scot in Northwest America / by
> Bruce Le Roy ; foreword by Robert Hitchman.—[s.l.] : pub-
> lished for the Washington State American Revolution
> Bicentennial Commission by the Washington State Historical
> Society and the Center for Northwest Folklore, c1978.—xx, 124
> p. : ill.   **F855.2.S3 L4**
>> Bibliography: p. 101–106.

219.

MacLean, J.P. (John Patterson), 1848–1939.

An historical account of the settlements of Scotch Highlanders in America prior to the peace of 1783 : together with notices of Highland regiments and biographical sketches.—Baltimore : Genealogical Pub. Co., 1968.—xiv, 455 p. : ill., port.

E184.S3 M2 1968

The "Historical Account" was originally published in Cleveland by Helman-Taylor Co. in 1900.

220.

Meyer, Duane Gilbert, 1926–

The Highland Scots of North Carolina, 1732–1776.—Chapel Hill : University of North Carolina Press, [1961].—viii, 218 p. : maps, diagrs. **F265.S3 M4 1961**

Bibliography: p. [194]–204.

221.

Newman, Harry Wright, 1894–

To Maryland from overseas : a complete digest of the Jacobite Loyalists sold into white slavery in Maryland and the British and Continental background of approximately 1400 Maryland settlers from 1634 to the early Federal Period with source documentation / by Harry Wright Newman.—Annapolis : H. W. Newman, 1982.—v, 190 p. **F190.S3 N48 1982**

Reprinted in Baltimore by Genealogical Pub. Co. in 1985.

ERRAND GIRL   FARMER'S DAUGHTER   MARKET WOMAN   WINTER COSTUME   LLANARTH GIRL

WELSH COSTUMES.

Published by T. Catherall, Chester.

Welsh costumes from Llandudno, Wales around 1850–1860. Illustrated in *Views of Llandudno and Its Neighbourhood*, Chester and Bangor : T. Catherall, 185–?, DA745.L7C3, last plate in vol. Library of Congress.

Chapter Three

Sources for Research in

elsh

Genealogy

CONTENTS

Handbooks

222.
Hamilton–Edwards, Gerald Kenneth Savery, 1906–
In search of Welsh ancestry / Gerald Hamilton-Edwards.—
Baltimore : Genealogical Pub. Co., 1986.—xi, 95 p. : ill.
CS452.H35 1986
Bibliography: p. 83–87.

223.
Welsh family history : a guide to research / edited by John
Rowlands and others.—[Aberystwyth] : Association of Family
History Societies of Wales, c1993.—xi, 316 p. : ill., facsims.,
maps. **CS453.W45 1993**
Includes bibliographical references (p. [298]–309) and index.
Reprinted in Baltimore by Genealogical Pub. Co. in 1994.

Pedigrees and Family Histories

224.
Bartrum, Peter C.
Early Welsh genealogical tracts / edited with notes and indexes
by P.C. Bartrum.—Cardiff : Wales U.P., 1966.—x, 228 p. 3
plates (facsims.) diagr. **CS456.B37**
Includes bibliographical references.

225.
Bartrum, Peter C.
Welsh genealogies, A.D. 300–1400 / Peter C. Bartrum.—
[Cardiff] : University of Wales Press [for] the Board of Celtic
Studies, 1974.—8 v. : geneal. tables. **CS456.B38 1974**
Contents: v. 1. Adam ab Ifor-Cydifor Fawr—v. 2. Cydrych-
Gosawl—v. 3. Grant-Malpas—v. 4. Marchudd-Yswatan
Wyddel—v. 5–8. Index.

226.
Bartrum, Peter C.
Welsh genealogies, A.D. 1400–1500 / Peter C. Bartrum.—
Aberystwyth : National Library of Wales, 1983.—18 v. :
genealogical tables, 1 map. **CS459.A2 B37 1983**

227.

Bradney, Joseph Alfred, *Sir,* **1859–.**

A history of Monmouthshire from the coming of the Normans into Wales down to the present time.—London : Mitchell, Hughes and Clarke, 1904–1933.—4 v. in 13 : ill. **DA670.M7 B8**

228.

Clark, George Thomas, 1809–1898.

Limbus patrum Morganifl et Glamorganifl. Being the genealogies of the older families of the lordships of Morgan and Glamorgan.—London : Wyman & sons, 1886.—2 p. leaves, 620 p. : fold. geneal. tables.   **Microfilm 8718 C <MicRR>**

229.

Glenn, Thomas Allen, 1864–.

Merion in the Welsh tract : with sketches of the townships of Haverford and Radnor. Historical and genealogical collections concerning the Welsh barony in the province of Pennsylvania, settled by the Cymric Quakers in 1682.—Norristown [Pa., : Herald Press.] 1896.—ix, 394 p., 1 leaf : ill. (incl. coats of arms) plates, facsims. (1 fold.).   **F159.M5 G5**

Reprinted in Baltimore by Genealogical Pub. Co. in 1970.

230.

Glenn, Thomas Allen.

Welsh founders of Pennsylvania.—Oxford : Fox, Jones and company, 1911–1913.—2 v. : ill. front. (v. 2) plates, ports., fold. tables.   **F160.W4 G5**

Reprinted in Baltimore by Genealogical Pub. Co. in 1970.

231.

Griffith, John Edwards.

Pedigrees of Anglesey and Carnarvonshire families, with their collateral branches in Denbighshire, Merionethshire and other parts / compiled by John Edward Griffith.—Horncastle, Eng. : printed for the author, by W. K. Morton and sons, ltd., 1914.— 3 p. leaves., 410 p.   **CS458.A6 G7**

Reprinted in Wrexham, Clwyd by Bridge Books in 1985.

232.

Jones, Francis.

The princes and principality of Wales.—Cardiff : University of Wales, 1969.—xxv, 204 p. : ill., coat of arms, tables, maps, port.

DA714.J58

Bibliography: p. xvii–xxv.

233.

Lloyd, Jacob Youde William, 1816–1887.

The history of the princes, the lords marcher, and the ancient nobility of Powys Fadog, and the ancient lords of Arwystli, Cedewen and Meirionydd.—London : T. Richards, 1881–1887.—6 v. : ill., plates, plans. **Microfilm 17654 CS**

234.

Nicholas, Thomas, 1820–1879.

Annals and antiquities of the counties and county families of Wales; containing a record of all ranks of the gentry.—London : Longmans, Green, Reader, & co., 1872.—2 v.

Microfilm 9132 (DA) <MicRR>

Reprinted in Baltimore by Genealogical Pub. Co. in 1991.

235.

Williams, John, fl. 1600.

Llyfr Baglan;.—London : Mitchell, Hughes and Clarke, 1910.—xii, 385 p. **CS458.B3 W5**

236.

Yorke, Philip, 1743–1804.

The royal tribes of Wales.—London : sold by B. Crosby and co., [1799].—192 p.: 12 ports.

DA708.Y65 <Rare Bk Coll : Pre-1801 Coll>
Microfilm 86/7070 (DA) <MicRR>

Bibliographies

237.

Blackwell, Henry, 1851–1928.

A bibliography of Welsh Americana / by Henry Blackwell.—2nd ed.—Aberystwyth : [National Library of Wales], 1977.—x, 126 p. **Z2071.B62 1977**

238.

Jack, R. I.

Medieval Wales / by R. Ian Jack.—Ithaca, N.Y. : Cornell University Press. [1972].—255 p.—(The Sources of history : studies in the uses of historical evidence). **Z2081.J3**

Includes bibliographical references.

239.

Jones, Philip Henry.

A bibliography of the history of Wales / compiled for the History and Law Committee of the University of Wales / by

Philip Henry Jones.—3rd ed.—Cardiff : University of Wales
Press, 1989.—75 p.   **Z2081.W229 1989**

Parish Registers

240.
Rawlins, Bert J.
The parish churches and nonconformist chapels of Wales : their
records and where to find them / by Bert J. Rawlins.—Salt Lake
City : Celtic Heritage Research, c1987–.—v. <1 > : ill., maps.
                                                CD1068.A2 R39 1987
Contents: v. 1. Carmarthenshire, Cardiganshire, and
Pembrokeshire—

241.
Williams, C.J. (Christopher John).
Cofrestri plwyf Cymru / cynullwyd gan C.J. Williams & J.
Watts-Williams = Parish registers of Wales / compiled by C.J.
Williams & J. Watts-Williams.—[Aberystwyth, Dyfed] :
National Library of Wales & Welsh County Archivists' Group
in association with the Society of Genealogists, 1986.—xxx, 217
p., [12] p. of plates : ill.   **CD1068.A2 W55 1986**

Local History

242.
The History of Wales.—Oxford : Clarendon Press ; Oxford ;
New York : Oxford University Press, 1981–<1988 >.—v. <2–4, 6
> : ill.   **DA714.H58 1981**
Includes bibliographies and indexes.
Contents:—v. 2. Conquest, coexistence, and change / by R.
R. Davies—v.3. Recovery, reorientation, and Reformation / by
Glanmor Williams—v. 4. The foundations of modern Wales /
by Geraint H. Jenkins—v. 6. Rebirth of a nation / by Kenneth
O. Morgan.

243.
Lhuyd, Edward, 1660–1709.
Parochialia : being a summary of answers to "Parochial queries
in order to a geographical dictionary, etc., of Wales" / issued by
Edward Lhwyd ; edited by Rupert H. Morris.—London :
Cambrian Archaeological Association, 1909–1911.—3 v. in 1 :
ill.—(Archaeologia cambrensis. Supplement ; Apr. 1909-
July 1911).   **DA734.L49 1909**

244.
Lloyd, John Edward, *Sir*, 1861–1947.
A history of Wales from the earliest times to the Edwardian conquest.—London : New York [etc.] Longmans, Green, and co., 1911.—2 v. : fold. map, geneal. tables.   DA715.L8

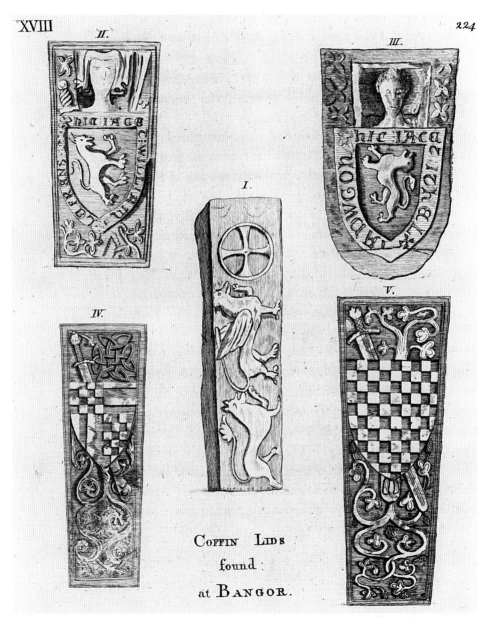

Ancient, heraldic coffin lids found in Bangor, Wales. Illustrated in *A Tour in Wales . . .* by Thomas Pennant, London: Printed for B. White, 1784, DA727.P41, vol. 1, plate XVIII, between p. 232 and p. 233. Library of Congress, Rare Book and Special Collections Division, Pre-1801 Collection.

Biographical Information

245.
The Dictionary of Welsh biography down to 1940 / under the auspices of the Honourable Society of Cymmrodorion ; [editors: John Edward Lloyd, R. T. Jenkins].—London, 1959.—lvii, 1157 p. : map.   **DA710.A1 B913**
  Bibliography: p. [xxxv]–lvii.

246.
Great Britain. Board of Education. Welsh Department.
  Famous Welshmen.—Cardiff : University of Wales Press Board, 1944.—141 p., 1 leaf.   **DA710.A1 G7 1944**

247.
Pughe, William Owen, 1759–1835.
  The Cambrian biography : or, Historical notices of celebrated men among the ancient Britons / by William Owen.—London : E. Williams, 1803.—2 p. leaves, vii, 345 p.   **DA716.A1 P9**
  Reprinted in New York by Garland in 1979.

248.
Rees, Thomas Mardy, 1861–.
  Notable Welshmen (1700–1900). . . with brief notes, in chronological order, and authorities.—Carnarvon : The "Herald" office, 1908.—xlii p., 1 leaf., 474, [6] p.   **DA710.A1 R5**

249.
Roberts, T. R.
  Eminent Welshmen: a short biographical dictionary of Welshmen who have attained distiction from earliest times to the present.—Cardiff & Merthyr Tydfil, The Educational publishing company, ltd., 1908–.—1 v. : front., ports.   **DA710.A1 R8**
  "The biographical dictionary of eminent Welshmen, by the Rev. Robert Williams, M.A. published in 1852 has long been out of print. The present dictionary brings that work up to date."—Pref.

250.
Rowland, E. H.
  A biographical dictionary of eminent Welshmen who flourished from 1700 to 1900 / by E. H. Rowland (Helen Elwy).—[Wrexham] : The authoress, 1907.—2 p. leaves, 295, [1] p.
                    DA710.A1 R85

251.

Salisbury, Enoch Robert Gibbon, 1819–1890.
>Border counties worthies / by E.G. Salisbury.—London [etc.] : Hodder and Stoughton [etc.], 1880.—2 pt. in 1 v. **DA740.B7 S2**

252.
>Who's who in Wales.—1st ed.—Cardiff : Western mail limited, 1921.—xxiv, 555, [1] p. **CT833.W5 1921**

Records

253.

Breese, Edward.
>Kalendars of Gwynedd : or, Chronological lists of lords-lieutenant, custodes rotulorum sheriffs and knights of the shire, for the counties of Anglesey, Caernarvon, and Merioneth, and of the members for the boroughs of Caernarvon and Beaumaris / comp. by Edward Breese ; with notes by William Watkin Edward Wynne.—London : J. C. Hotten, 1873.—vii p., 161 p. : col. front (facsim.). **DA700.B6**

254.

Great Britain. Public Record Office.
>Calendar of ancient petitions relating to Wales : thirteenth to sixteenth century / [held in the] Public Record Office ; edited with introduction by William Rees.—Cardiff : University of Wales Press, 1975.—xxxviii, 559 p. : map.—(Board of Celtic Studies, History and law series ; no. 28). **KD9430.C3**
>>Bibliography: p. [xxxvii]–xxxviii.

255.

Henson, Nia.
>Index of the probate records of the Bangor Consistory Court / compiled by Nia Henson.—Aberystwyth : National Library of Wales, <1980– >.—v. <1 >.—(N. L. W. probate indexes ; no. 1). **KD8688.B36 H46**
>An index to all the pre-1858 probate records housed in the National Library of Wales.
>>Contents: v. 1. Pre-1700—

256.
Jones, Francis, 1908–
> Report on the Welsh manuscripts contained in the muniments of the College of Arms / prepared by Francis Jones.—London : College of Arms, 1957.—54 leaves, [5] leaves of plates : maps.
> **Z5313.G69J66 1957**

257.
Jones, Nansi C.
> Archdeaconry of Brecon probate records / compiled by Nansi C. Jones.—Aberystwyth : National Library of Wales, <1989– >.—v. <1 >.—(National Library of Wales probate indexes ; no. 2). **CS453.J66 1989**
>> Includes bibliographical references and indexes.
>> Contents: v. 1. Pre-1660—

Maps, Atlases, Gazetteers

258.
Lewis, Samuel, d. 1865.
> A topographical dictionary of Wales, comprising the several counties, cities, boroughs, corporate and market towns, parishes, chapelries, and townships, with historical and statistical descriptions.—London, S. Lewis and co., 1833.—2 v. in 1. : ill. (coats of arms) maps (1 fold.). **DA734.L47**

259.
Rees, William, 1887–
> An historical atlas of Wales from early to modern times / by William Rees.—New ed.—London : Faber and Faber, 1972.—1 atlas (vii, 71 p., [71] p. of plates) : ill., maps (some col.).
> **G1821.S1 R4 1972 <G&M>**

260.
Richards, Melville.
> Welsh administrative and territorial units, medieval and modern.—Cardiff : University of Wales Press, 1969.—xviii, 228 p, 229–324 p. of 104 maps. **JS4012.L7 R5**

Names, Geographical

261.
Davies, Dewi.
> Welsh place-names and their meanings / by Dewi Davies.—
> [Brecon : The author, 1977].—60 p.   DA734.D38

262.
Morgan, Thomas.
> The place-names of Wales.—2d and rev. ed.—Newport. Mon., :
> J. E. Southall, 1912.—2 p. leaves, 262 p.   DA734.M7

263.
Wales. University. Board of Celtic Studies, Language and Literature Committee.
> Rhestr o enwau lleoedd.—3. arg.—Caerdydd : Gwasg Prifysgol
> Cymru, 1967.—xxxvii, 119 p. : 2 maps, diagr.
> DA734.W3 1967

Names, Personal

264.
Davies, Trefor Rendall.
> A book of Welsh names.—London : Sheppard Press, [1952].—
> 72 p.   PB2183.D3

265.
Lasker, Gabriel Ward.
> Atlas of British surnames : with 154 maps of selected surnames
> / G. W. Lasker, C. G. N. Mascie-Taylor.—Detroit : published
> for the Guild of One-Name Studies by Wayne State University
> Press, [1990].—x, 86 p. : maps.   CS2507.L37 1990
> Includes bibliographical references (p. 7–8) and index.

266.
Morgan, T. J.
> Welsh surnames / by T. J. Morgan and Prys Morgan.—Cardiff :
> University of Wales Press, 1985.—211 p. : ill.
> CS2445.M67 1985
> Bibliography: p. [206]–211.

267.
Rowlands, John.
The surnames of Wales for family historians and others / John Rowlands, Sheila Rowlands.—Baltimore : Genealogical Pub. Co., 1996.—217 p. **CS2445.R69 1996**

Periodicals

268.
Archaeologia cambrensis, the journal of the Cambrian archaeological association.—[Vol. 1, no. 1] (Jan. 1846)– . [London : W. Pickering, 1846–]. **DA700 .A66**
Irregular.
Title varies. Some indexes available, see NUC. Vols. for 1850–1854 called new ser., v. 1–5; 1855–1869 called 3rd ser., v. 1–14; 1870–1883 called 4th ser., v. 1–17; 1884–1900 called 5th ser., v. 1–20; 1921–1928 called 7th ser., v. 1–8, and also called v. 76–83; 1929– v. 84–.

269.
Bye-gones, relating to Wales and the border counties.—2nd ser. Vol. 1 (1889)– .—Oswestry : printed at the Caxton works, 1889–
DA700.B9

270.
Y Cymmrodor, embodying the transactions of the Cymmrodorion Society of London.—Vol. 1, pt. 1 (Jan. 1877)–[Vol. 50 (1951?)].—[London] : The Society, 1877–[1951]. **DA700.C9**
Title varies. In later years individual contributions comprise the entire volume.
Not published 1879.

271.
Honourable Society of Cymmrodorion (London, England).
The transactions of the Honourable Society of Cymmrodorion.—Session 1892/93–.—London : The Society, 1893–.—
DA700.C94
Annual.
Index to 1–23, 1877–1912 in its 1911/12 issue which includes index to *Y Cymmrodor, Embodying the Transactions of the Honourable Society of Cymmrodorion of London*, v. 1–6, 1877–1883, and *Y Cymmrodor*, v. 7–23, 1883–1912. Previous to 1892 the *Transactions* were included in *Y Cymmrodor*.

272.
Old Wales : a monthly magazine of antiquities for Wales and the borders.—3 v. 1905–1907.—Talybont, Breconshire : "Old Wales" office, 1905–1907.— DA700.O6

273.
South Wales and Monmouth Record Society.
Publications.—[1932]– .—[Cardiff : W. Lewis (Printers), 1932]– DA700 .S62

274.
West Wales historical records. The annual magazine of the Historical society of West Wales.—Vol. 1–14, 1910–1929.— Carmarthen : Printed by W. Spurrell & son, 1912–1929
DA700.W5
Annual.

Religions

275.
The American Baptist heritage in Wales / edited by Carroll C. and Willard A. Ramsey.—Lafayette, Tenn. : Church History Research and Archives Affiliation, 1976.—xxii, 121, ix, 76 p. : ill. BX6291.A43

276.
Great Britain. General Register Office.
The Religious Census of 1851, a calendar of the returns relating to Wales.—Cardiff : University of Wales Press, 1976–1981.—2 v. : facsims.—(History and law series ; no. 30–31). BR773.G7 1976
Contents: v. 1. South Wales—v. 2. North Wales.

Welsh in the United States

277.
Ashton, E. T. (Elwyn Thomas).
> The Welsh in the United States / by Elwyn T. Ashton.—Hove,
> Sussex : Caldra House, 1984.—182 p. : ill. **E184.W4 A84 1984**
>> Bibliography: p. 175–176.

278.
Browning, Charles Henry.
> Welsh settlement of Pennsylvania.—Philadelphia : W.J.
> Campbell, 1912.—631, [1] p. : ill., maps, front., plates.
>> **F160.W4 B8**
>> Reprinted in Baltimore by Genealogical Pub. Co. in 1967.

279.
Dennis, Ronald D., 1940–
> The call of Zion : the story of the first Welsh Mormon emigra-
> tion / Ronald D. Dennis.—Provo, Utah : Religious Studies
> Center, Brigham Young University, 1987.—xii, 243 p. : ill.—
> (Religious Studies Center specialized monograph series ; v. 2).
>> **E184.M8 D46 1987**
>> Bibliography: p. 241–243.

280.
Hartmann, Edward George, 1912–
> Americans from Wales.—Boston : Christopher Pub. House.
> [1967].—291 p.   **E184.W4 H33**
>> Bibliography: p. 225–267.

281.
Thomas, R. D. (Robert David), 1817–1888.
> Hanes Cymry America = A history of the Welsh in America /
> R. D. Thomas ; translated by Phillips G. Davies.—Lanham,
> Md. : University Press of America, c1983.—xxi, 517 p.
>> **E184.W4 T413 1983**
>> Includes bibliographies.

O'Rourke's Tower and great Cross in sacred Clonmacnoise, Ireland, 1905. LC–USZ62–112329, Foreign Geographical File, Stereograph Collection. Library of Congress, Prints and Photographs Division.

Chapter Four

Sources for Research in

rish

Genealogy

CONTENTS

Handbooks

282.

Edwards, R. Dudley (Robert Dudley), 1909–

Sources for early modern Irish history, 1534–1641 / R. W. Dudley Edwards and Mary O'Dowd.—Cambridge [Cambridgeshire] ; New York : Cambridge University Press, 1985.—x, 222 p.—(The Sources of history, studies in the uses of historical evidence). **DA905.E38 1985**

Includes bibliographical references and index.

283.

Falley, Margaret Dickson, 1898–

Irish and Scotch-Irish ancestral research : a guide to the genealogical records, methods and sources in Ireland.— Evanston, Ill. : [s.n., 1962].—2 v. **CS483.F32**

Contents: v. 1. Repositories and records—v. 2. Bibliography and family index.

Reprinted in Baltimore by Genealogical Pub. Co. in 1981.

284.

Glynn, Joseph Martin, 1932–

Manual for Irish genealogy : a guide to methods and sources for tracing Irish ancestry / compiled by Joseph Martin Glynn, Jr.— 2nd ed., rev., corr. & enl.—Newton, Mass. : Irish Family History Society, c1982.—1 v. (various pagings) : ill.

CS483.G58 1982

Includes bibliographical references.

285.

Grenham, John.

Tracing your Irish ancestors : the complete guide / John Grenham.—Dublin : Gill and Macmillan, c1992.—xxxviii, 281 p. : maps. **CS483.G74 1992**

Reprinted in Baltimore by Genealogical Pub. Co. in 1993.

286.

Handbook on Irish genealogy : how to trace your ancestors and relatives in Ireland.—6th ed. / rev. and edited by Donal F. Begley.—Dublin, Ireland : Heraldic Artists, 1984.—155, [5] p. : ill.—(Heraldry and genealogy series). **CS483.H36 1984**

287.

Irish genealogy : a record finder / edited by Donal F. Begley.— Dublin, Ireland : Heraldic Artists, c1987.—252 p.—(Heraldry and genealogy series). **CS484.I75 1987**

"Miscellaneous genealogical sources": p. 241–248.

288.
McCarthy, Tony.
> The Irish roots guide / Tony McCarthy.—Dublin : Lilliput,
> 1991.—ix, 116 p. : ill.   **CS483.M28 1991**
> Includes bibliographical references (p. 113–116).

289.
Mitchell, Brian S.
> Pocket guide to Irish genealogy / Brian Mitchell.—Baltimore :
> Genealogical Pub. Co., 1991.—63 p.   **CS483.M57 1991**

290.
> A New history of Ireland / edited by T. W. Moody, F. X.
> Martin, F. J. Byrne.—Oxford [England] : Clarendon Press ;
> New York : Oxford University Press, <1976–1989 >.—v. <2–5,
> 8–9 > : ill.   **DA912.N48**
>> Includes bibliographies and indexes.
>> Contents:—v. 2. Medieval Ireland, 1169–1534—v. 3. Early
>> modern Ireland, 1534–1691—v. 4. Eighteenth-century Ireland,
>> 1691–1800—v. 5. Ireland under the Union, I, 1801–1870—v. 8.
>> A chronology of Irish history to 1976—v. 9. Maps, genealogies,
>> lists—

291.
O'Laughlin, Michael C.
> The complete book for tracing your Irish ancestors / by Michael
> C. O'Laughlin.—Kansas City, Mo. : Irish Genealogical
> Foundation, c1980.—224 p. : ill., maps.   **CS49.O25**
> Includes bibliographical references.

292.
Reakes, Janet.
> How to trace your Irish ancestors : an A-Z approach / Janet
> Reakes.—Sydney, NSW : Hale & Iremonger, c1987.—64 p. :
> ill., maps.   **CS483.R43 1987**

293.
Ryan, James G., 1950–
> Irish records : sources for family & local history / by James G.
> Ryan.—Salt Lake City : Ancestry Pub., c1988.—li, 562 p. : ill.,
> maps.   **Z5313.I7 R83 1988**
>> Includes bibliographies and index.

294.
Yurdan, Marilyn.
> Irish family history / Marilyn Yurdan.—Baltimore : Genealogical
> Pub. Co., 1990.—xii, 194 p. : ill.   **CS483.Y87 1990**
>> Includes bibliographical references (p. 187–191) and index.

Pedigrees and Family Histories ❧

295.
Black, J. Anderson.
Your Irish ancestors / by J. Anderson Black.—[New York] :
Paddington Press, [1974].—253 p. : ill.   **CS483.B55**
    Bibliography: p. 250–251.

296.
Burke's Irish family records / [editor, Hugh Montgomery-
Massingberd].—London : Burke's Peerage Limited ; New York
: Distributed in North America by Arco Pub. Co., 1976.—xxxii,
1237 p.—(Burke's series).   **CS482.B87 1976**
    Revision of *Burke's Landed Gentry of Ireland.* 1958.

297.
Curtis, Edmund, 1881–
A history of medieval Ireland from 1086 to 1513.—London :
Methuen & co., ltd., [1938].—xxxv, 433, [1] p. : incl. geneal.
tables, maps (1 fold.).   **DA933.C8 1938**
    This "enlarged and completely rewritten" edition was
reprinted in New York by Barnes and Noble in 1968.

298.
D'Alton, John, 1792–1867.
Illustrations, historical and genealogical, of King James's Irish
army list, 1689.—2nd ed.—London : J. R. Smith, 1861.—2 v.
          DA945.D15

299.
Durning, William P.
A guide to Irish roots : collected from oral tradition and ancient
records during visits to Ireland, other parts of Europe, and North
America / by William and Mary Durning ; photos by the
authors, cover by Clayton Clark III, art by Wendi Fitzpatrick.—
La Mesa, Calif. : Irish Family Names Society, 1986.—viii, 77,
154, 47 p., [2] p. of plates : ill.   **CS483.D87 1986**

300.
Durning, William P.
If you're a wee bit Irish : a chart of old Irish families collected
from folk tradition / [by Ulliam O'Duirnin, i.e. W. P.
Durning].—La Mesa, Calif. : Irish Family Names Society,
1978.—xxvi, 166 p. : geneal. tables.   **CS484.D87**
    Bibliography: p. 163–165.

301.

Jones, Henry Z., 1940–

The Palatine families of Ireland / Henry Z. Jones.—2nd ed.—
Camden, Me. : Picton Press, 1990.—xvii, 166 p. : ill.

CS496.P3 J6 1990

Includes bibliographical references (p. 149–151) and index.

302.

Keating, Geoffrey, 1570?–1644?

The history of Ireland, from the earliest period to the English
invasion : with a map showing the location of the ancient clans,
and a topographical appendix = Foras feasa ar Eirinn do réir an
athar seathrun ceiting, ollamh ré diadhachta / by Geoffrey
Keating ; translated from the original Gaelic and copiously
annotated by John O'Mahony.—Kansas City, Mo. : Irish
Genealogical Foundation, c1983.—3 v. (782 p.): ill.

DA930.K2513 1983

Originally published in New York by P. M. Haverty in 1857.

303.

O'Hart, John.

The Irish and Anglo-Irish landed gentry when Cromwell came
to Ireland ; or, A supplement to Irish pedigrees.—Dublin :
M.H. Gill & son, 1884.—xvii, [1], 773, [1] p.

Microfilm 8859 CS

Microfilm. Washington, D.C., Library of Congress.
Reprinted in New York by Barnes and Noble in 1969
(**CS490.O5 1969**); facsimile reprint published in Shannon by
Irish University Press in 1969.   (**CS490.O5 1884a**)

304.

O'Hart, John.

Irish pedigrees; or The origin and stem of the Irish nation.—5th
ed.—Dublin; J. Duffy and co. ltd. ; New York : Benziger
Brothers, 1892.—2 v.   **CS483.O5**

Reprinted in Baltimore by Genealogical Pub. Co. in 1976.

305.

Rooney, John, 1837–

A genealogical history of Irish families with their crests and
armorial bearings.—[New York : Cherouny printing and publishing co., 1896].—531, vi p. : ill., plates (partly col.) ports.,
coats of arms.   **CS498.R7**

Bibliographies

306.
Asplin, P. W. A., 1939–
Medieval Ireland, c. 1170–1495 : a bibliography of secondary works, by P. W. A. Asplin.—Dublin : Royal Irish Academy, 1971.—xv, 139 p.—(A New history of Ireland. Ancillary publications, no. 1). **Z2041.A85**

307.
Blessing, Patrick J.
The Irish in America : a guide to the literature and the manuscript collections / Patrick J. Blessing.—Washington : Catholic University of America Press, c1992.—xi, 347 p.
Z1361.I7 B54 1992

308.
De Breffny, Brian.
Bibliography of Irish family history and genealogy / compiled and edited by Brian de Breffny.—Cork : Golden Eagle Books, 1974, c1973.—167 p. **Z5313.I7 D4**

309.
Eager, Alan R.
A guide to Irish bibliographical material : a bibliography of Irish bibliographies and sources of information / Alan R. Eager.— 2nd rev. and enl. ed.—Westport, Conn. : Greenwood Press, 1980.—xv, 502 p. **Z2031.E16 1980**

310.
Evans, Edward, d. 1901.
Historical and bibliographical account of almanacks, directories, etc., etc., published in Ireland from the sixteenth century: their rise, progress, and decay, with jottings of their compilers and printers. A book for the antiquary as well as the general reader / by Edward Evans.—Dublin : Office of "The Irish builder," 1897.—viii, 149, [1] p. **Z2039.A6 E8**
Facsimile edition, with an introduction by Thomas Wall published in Blackrock by Carraig Books in 1976.

311.
Hayes, Richard J., 1902–
Sources for the history of Irish civilisation : articles in Irish periodicals / edited by Richard J. Hayes.—Boston : G.K. Hall, 1970.—9 v. **Z2034.H35**
Contents: v. 1–5. Persons—v. 6–8. Subjects.—v. 9. Places-Dates.

312.

Lester, DeeGee.

Irish research : a guide to collections in North America, Ireland, and Great Britain / compiled by DeeGee Lester.—New York : Greenwood Press, 1987.—xvi, 348 p.—(Bibliographies and indexes in world history, 0742–6852 ; no. 9).   **Z2031.L47 1987**

Companion to *Immigrants from Great Britain and Ireland* / Jack W. Weaver and DeeGee Lester.

313.

MacLysaght, Edward.

Bibliography of Irish family history / Edward MacLysaght.— 2nd ed.—Blackrock, County Dublin, Ireland : Irish Academic Press, 1982.—71 p.   **Z5313.I7 M32 1982**

314.

Martin, G. H. (Geoffrey Haward), 1928–

A bibliography of British and Irish municipal history [by] G. H. Martin and Sylvia McIntyre.—Leicester : Leicester University Press ; distributed by Humanities Press, New York, 1972–.—v. ‹1 ›.   **Z2023.M26**

Contents: v. 1. General works—

315.

National Library of Ireland.

Manuscript sources for the history of Irish civilisation / edited by Richard J. Hayes.—Boston : G.K. Hall, 1965.—11 v.

Z2041.D85

———— ———— First supplement, 1965–1975 / compiled in the National Library of Ireland.—Boston : G. K. Hall, 1979.—v. ‹1–3 ›.   **Z2041.D85 Suppl. ‹fol.›**

Incomplete Contents: v. 1. Persons—v. 2. Subjects. Places— v. 3. Dates. Lists of manuscripts—

316.

Subject guide to books / general editor, Lionel R. McColvin ; associate editors, K. R. McColvin [and] E. W. Padwick.— London : J. Clarke, [‹1959– ›—v. ‹ 1–3 ›].   **Z1035.L68**

Contents: v. 1. History, travel & description—v. 2. Biography, family history, heraldry, genealogy, etc.—v. 3. Language and literature—

Local History

317.
Great Britain. Ordnance Survey of Ireland.

Letters written by John O'Donovan containing information relative to the history and antiquities of counties in Ireland collected during the progress of the ordnance survey from 1834–1841.—Bray, Ireland : [s.n.], 1927–1934.—   **DA905.A4**

Contents: Contents: I. Calvan & Leitrim (Breifny), 1836—II. Clare, 1839, Pts. 1, 2, & 3—III. Donegal. 1835—IV. Down. 1834—V. Dublin. 1837—VI. Fermanagh. 1834–35—VII. Galway. 1839, Pts. 1, 2, & 3—VIII. Kerry. 1841—IX. Kildare. 1837, Kilkenny. 1839—X. King's County. 1839—XI. Limerick. 1840. Pts. 1 & 2—XII. Londonderry. 1834—XIII. Longford. 1838—XIV. Louth. 1835–1836—XV. Mayo. 1838, Pts. 1 & 2—XVI. Meath. 1836—XVII. Queen's County. 1838—XVIII. Roscommon. 1837—XIX. Sligo. 1836—XX. Tipperary. 1840, Pts. 1 & 2—XXI. Waterford. 1841—XXII. Westmeath. 1837—XXIII. Wexford. 1840.

318.
Irish free state. Irish manuscripts commission.

The civil survey.—Dublin : Stationery Office, 1931–1961.—10 v. : maps.   **HD624.A45**

Contents: I. County of Tipperary. Eastern and southern baronies—II. County of Tipperary. Western and northern baronies, with the return of crown and church lands for the whole county—III. Counties of Donegal, Londonderry and Tyrone, with the returns of church lands for the three counties—IV. County of Limerick, with a section of Clanmaurice barony, co. Kerry—V. County of Meath, with returns of tithes for the Meath baronies—VI. County of Waterford. With appendices: Muskerry barony, co. Cork, Kilkenny city and liberties (part) also valuations, circa 1663–1664, for Waterford and Cork cities.—VII. County of Dublin—VIII. County of Kildare—IX. County of Wexford—X. Miscellanea.

319.
Nolan, William.

Tracing the past : sources for local studies in the Republic of Ireland / [by William Nolan].—Dublin : Geography Publications, 1982.—x, 149 p. : ill.   **DA905.N643 1982**

Bibliography: p. 130–146.

320.

Ordnance survey memoirs of Ireland / edited by Angélique Day and Patrick McWilliams.—Belfast : Institute of Irish Studies in association with the Royal Irish Academy, Dublin, 1990–<c1996 >.—v. <1–35 > : ill., maps.   **DA990.U46 O85 1990**

Contents: v. 1. Parishes of County Armagh, 1835–8—v. 2. Parishes of County Antrim (i), 1838–9—v. 3. Parishes of County Down I, 1834–6—v. 4. Parishes of County Fermanagh I, 1834–5—v. 5. Parishes of County Tyrone I, 1821, 1823, 1831–6—v. 6. Parishes of County Londonderry I, 1830, 1834, 1836—v. 7. Parishes of County Down II, 1832–4, 1837—v. 8. Parishes of County Antrim II, 1832–8—v. 9. Parishes of County Londonderry II, 1833–5—v. 10. Parishes of County Antrim III, 1833, 1835, 1839–40—v. 11. Parishes of County Londonderry III, 1831–5—v. 12. Parishes of County Down III, 1833–8—v. 13. Parishes of County Antrim IV, 1830–8—v. 14. Parishes of County Fermanagh II, 1834–5—v. 15. Parishes of County Londonderry IV, 1824, 1833–5—v. 16. Parishes of County Antrim V, 1830–5, 1837–8—v. 17. Parishes of County Down IV, 1833–7—v. 18. Parishes of County Londonderry V, 1830, 1833, 1836–7—v. 19. Parishes of County Antrim VI, 1830, 1833, 1835–8—v. 20. Parishes of County Tyrone II, 1825, 1833–5, 1840—v. 21. Parishes of County Antrim VII, 1832–8—v. 22. Parishes of County Londonderry VI, 1831, 1833, 1835–6—v. 23. Parishes of County Antrim VIII, 1831–5, 1837–8, Ballymena and West Antrim—v. 24. Parishes of County Antrim IX, 1830–1832, 1835, 1838–1839—v. 25. Parishes of County Londonderry VII, 1834–1835. North-West Londonderry—v. 26. Parishes of County Antrim X, 1830–1, 1833–5, 1983–40—v. 27. Parishes of County Londonderry VIII, 1830, 1833–7, 1839. East Londonderry—v. 28. Parishes of County Londonderry IX, 1832–8. West Londonderry—v. 29. Parishes of County Antrim XI, 1832–3, 1835–9. Antrim town and Ballyclare—v. 30. Parishes of County Londonderry X, 1833–5, 1838. Mid-Londonderry—v. 31. Parishes of County Londonderry XI, 1821–1833, 1836–7. South Londonderry— v. 32. Parishes of County Antrim XII, 1832–3, 1835–40. Ballynure and district—v. 33. Parishes of County Londonderry XII, 1829–30, 1832, 1834–36. Coleraine and Mouth of the Bann—v. 34. Parishes of County Londonderry XIII, 1831–8. Clondermot and the Waterside—v. 35. Parishes of County Antrim XIII, 1833, 1835, 1838. Templepatrick and district.

Biographical Information

321.

Ball, Francis Erlington, d. 1928.
> The judges in Ireland, 1221–1921.—London : J. Murray,
> [1926].—2 v. : fronts.   LAW <**Great Britain Ireland 7 "Ball"**>
>> Reprinted in Blackrock, Co. Dublin, Ireland and Portland,
> Ore. by Round Hall Press in 1993.   **(KDK1652.B34 1993)**

322.

Boylan, Henry.
> A dictionary of Irish biography / Henry Boylan.—2nd ed.—
> New York : St. Martin's Press, 1988.—420 p.   **CT862.B69 1988**
>> Bibliography: p. [413]–420.

323.

Brown, Stephen J. M. (Stephen James Meredith), 1881–1962.
> International index of Catholic biographies / compiled by Stephen
> J. Brown.—2nd ed., rev. and greatly enl.—London : Burns, Oates
> and Washbourne, 1935.—2 p. leaves, [vii]–xix, 287 p.—(Catholic
> bibliographical series ; no. 3 (i.e. 2).   **Z7837.B88 1935**
>> Contents: pt. I. General biographical reference-books—
> pt. II. Collective biography.

324.

Cairnduff, Maureen.
> Who's who in Ireland : the influential 1,000 / edited by
> Maureen Cairnduff.—Updated 2nd ed.—Dun Laoghaire, Co.
> Dublin : Hibernian Pub. Co., c1991.—249 p. : ill.
>> **CT862.C35 1991**

325.

Campbell, John Hugh.
> History of the Friendly Sons of St. Patrick and of the Hibernian
> Society for the Relief of Emigrants from Ireland.—Philadelphia
> : The Hibernian Society, 1892.—570 p. : ill., col. front., ports.,
> facsims.   **F158.9.I6 S65**

326.

Coffey, Hubert William.

Irish families in Australia and New Zealand, 1788–1978 / by Hubert William Coffey and Marjorie Jean Morgan.—1st. ed.— South Melbourne, Vic. : H.W. Coffey, 1978–1980.—4 v.

CS2008.A1 C63

Contents: v. 1. A–D—v. 2. E–K—v. 3. L–Q—v. 4. R–Z.

327.

Crone, John S. (John Smyth), 1858–1945.

A concise dictionary of Irish biography / by John S. Crone.— Rev. and enl. ed.—Dublin ; The Talbot press, 1937.—viii, 290 p. **DA916.C7 1937**

"Authorities": p. vi–vii.

328.

Loeber, Rolf.

A biographical dictionary of architects in Ireland, 1600–1720 / Rolf Loeber.—London : J. Murray, 1981.—127 p.

NA987.L63 1981

Includes bibliographical references and index.

329.

Ryan, Richard, 1796–1849.

Biographia hibernica.—London : R. Ryan, 1819–21.—2 v. : front. (port.). **DA916.R9**

330.

Thom's Irish who's who : a biographical book of reference of prominent men and women in Irish life at home and abroad.— [Vol. 1] (1923)– .—Dublin : A. Thom & co., ltd.; London : D. O'Connor, 1923–. **DA916.T5**

331.

Trinity College (Dublin, Ireland).

Alumni dublinenses : a register of the students, graduates, professors and provosts of Trinity college in the University of Dublin (1593–1860) / edited by the late George Dames Burtchaell and Thomas Ulick Sadleir.—New ed. (with supplement).—Dublin : A. Thom & co., ltd., 1935.—2. p.leaves, vii–xiii p., l leaf, xv–xiix, 905, [1], 148 p. : ill., front. (port.).

LF904.A2 A3 1593–1860

Bibliography: p. xv–xvi.

332.

Webb, Alfred John, 1834–1908.

A compendium of Irish biography.—Dublin : M. H. Gill & son, 1878.—xix, 598 p. **DA916.W3**

Reprinted in New York by Lemma Pub. Corp. in 1970.

Land, Property, and Other Records

333.
Alphabetical index to the names contained in the premium entitlement lists of the trustees of the linen and hempen manufactures of Ireland : also known by the short title: 1796 spinning wheel survey of Ireland.—Vienna, Va. : All-Ireland Heritage, c1986.—12 microfiches.—(All-Ireland Heritage microfiche series). **Microfiche 88/278 (D) <MicRR>**

334.
Directory of Irish archives / edited by Seamus Helferty and Raymond Refausse.—2nd ed.—Blackrock, Co. Dublin : Irish Academic Press, 1993.—154 p. **CD1101.D57 1993**

335.
Dublin. National Library of Ireland.
Irish genealogy.—Dublin : Genealogical Society of the Church of Jesus Christ of Latter-Day Saints, 1949.
Microfilm 1616 , 1617 CS
For an explanation and index see Anne Toohey's *Irish Genealogical Office Manuscripts: A Guide to the Microfilm* (Library of Congress, Humanities and Social Sciences Division, 1993, LH&G Ref Desk).

336.
General valuation of ratetable property in Ireland / Richard Griffith.—Dublin, Ireland : Irish Microforms Ltd., c1978.—472 microfiches ; 11 x 15 cm. **Microfiche (w) 89/9001 (D) <MicRR>**
Title on microfiche header: *Griffith's valuation.*

337.
Ireland. Local Government Board.
Land owners in Ireland. Return of owners of land of one acre and upwards, in the several counties, counties of cities, and counties of towns in Ireland.—Dublin : H.M. Stationery Off., 1876.—vi, 325 p. **HD1206.G8 S7 1874 (law)**
Reprinted in Baltimore by Genealogical Pub. Co. in 1988 **(HD625.L19 1988).**

338.
Ireland. Public Record Office.
Report of the deputy keeper of the public records in Ireland.—Vol. 1 (1869)– .—Dublin : Printed by Alexander Thom, ltd., [1869– **DA905.I66**

339.

Irish Manuscripts Commission.

Books of survey and distribution : being abstracts of various surveys and instruments of title, 1636–1703 / prepared for publication with introductory notes by Robert C. Simington.—Dublin : Stationary Office, <1949–1967 >.—v. <1–4 > : fold. maps (part in pocket). **DA905.A53**

Contents: v. 1. County of Roscommon—v. 2. County of Mayo—v. 3. County of Galway—v. 4. County of Clare.

340.

Irish Manuscripts Commission.

A census of Ireland, circa 1659 ; with supplementary material from the poll money ordinances (1660–1661) / edited by Seamus Pender.—Dublin : Stationary office, 1939.—2 p. leaves, xix, 946 p. : incl. tables. **HA1142 1659**

341.

Northern Ireland. Public Record Office.

Annual reports of the Deputy Keeper of Public Records in Ireland : reports 1 to 56, 1869 to 1931.—Dublin, Ireland : Irish Microforms Ltd., c1978.—96 microfiches ; 11 x 15 cm. **Microfiche 6002 (D) <MicRR>**

Title on microfiche header: Public records in Ireland : reports.

342.

Northern Ireland. Public Record Office.

Report.—1925– .—Belfast, 1925– **CD1117.N6 A3**
Annual.

343.

Pfeiffer, Betty.

Ireland—the Householder's index, the Griffith's valuation / Betty Pfeiffer.—[S.l.] : B. Pfeiffer, 1988.—75 p. : ill. **CS484.P48 1988**

344.

The Tithe applotment books.—[Dublin?] : European Micropublishing Services, 1990.—145 microfilm reels ; 35 mm. **Microfilm 93/186 (C) <MicRR>**

Microfilmed from the collection of the National Archives of Ireland.

GUIDE: Accompanied by a printed guide and index, MicRR Guide No.: 293.

Tithes were taxes in kind, such as corn or hay, levied from 1823 to 1832.

Maps, Atlases, Gazetteers

345.

Bartholomew, John, 1831–1893.

Philip's 19th century county atlas of Ireland / with original consulting index and edited with a new introduction by John D. Blackwell & Laurie C. C. Stanley Blackwell.—Kingston, Canada : Cluny Press, 1984.—1 atlas (58 p.) : ill., maps.

G1830.B33 1984 <G&M>

Reprint with new introd. Originally published as *Philip's Handy Atlas of the Counties of Ireland* / John Bartholomew ; rev. by P. W. Joyce. London : G. Philip, 1881. List of addresses for further research: p. 58.

Bibliography: p. xii–xiv.

346.

Carlisle, Nicholas.

A topographical dictionary of Ireland.—London : printed for W. Miller by W. Savage, 1810.—xxix, [705] p.   DA979.C28

Bibliography: p. [xvii]–xix.

347.

Hansbrow, G. *Rev.*

An improved topographical and historical Hibernian gazetteer . . . scientifically arranged, with an appendix of ancient names.—Dublin : R. M. Tims, 1835.—xiv, [15]–431, [1] p.

DA979.H24

348.

Leet, Ambrose.

A directory to the market towns, villages, gentlemen's seats, and other noted places in Ireland.—2nd ed.—Dublin : printed by B. Smith, 1814.—4, 394, [56] p.   DA975.L48

349.

Lewis, Samuel, d. 1865.

Lewis's Atlas comprising the countries of Ireland, and a general map of the kingdom.—London : S. Lewis & co. 1837.—2 p. leaves, 33 col. maps on 33 leaves, (1 fold.).

G1830.L4 1837 <G&M>

350.

Lewis, Samuel, d. 1865.

A topographical dictionary of Ireland : comprising the several counties, cities, boroughs, corporate, market, and post towns, parishes, and villages, with historical and statistical descriptions . . . / by Samuel Lewis.—Baltimore : Genealogical Pub. Co., 1984.—2 v. : coats of arms.   **DA979.L48 1984**

"Originally published: London, 1837"—T.p. verso.

351.
Mason, William Shaw, 1774–1853.
A statistical account, or parochial survey of Ireland drawn up from the communications of the clergy / [by William S. Mason].—Dublin : printed by Graisberry and Campbell, for J. Cumming, 1814–19.—3 v. : 15 plates, 20 maps, 4 plans.
                    DA975.M39

352.
Miller, James, of New York.
Reference book of Ireland.—New York : Cooke & Cobb, 1877.—11 p. leaves, [1], 148, [4] p. : 5 plates, fold. map.
                    DA979.M65

353.
Mitchell, Brian.
A new genealogical atlas of Ireland / Brian Mitchell.—Baltimore : Genealogical Pub. Co., 1986.—1 atlas (123 p.) : maps.   **G1831.F7 M5 1986 <G&M>**

Shows counties, baronies, civil parishes, dioceses, poor law unions, and probate districts; links these with major record sources of Ireland. "It is intended that this volume of maps be used in conjunction with the '*General alphabetical index to the townlands and towns, parishes, and baronies of Ireland*' (Alexander Thom, Dublin, 1861; repr. by Genealogical Publishing Company, Baltimore, 1984)."—Introd.

Bibliography: p. 10.

354.
Parish maps of Ireland : (depicting all townlands in the four Ulster counties of Armagh, Donegal, Londonderry, and Tyrone) / compiled by The Derry Youth and Community Workshop under the direction of Brian Mitchell.—Apollo, Pa. : Closson Press, 1988.—1 atlas (287 p. (some fold.)) : maps.
                    G1833.U4 E423 P3 1988 <G&M>

355.
The Parliamentary gazetteer of Ireland, adapted to the new poor-law, franchise, municipal and ecclesiastical arrangements, and compiled with a special reference to the lines of railroad and canal communication, as existing in 1844–45.—Dublin : A. Fullarton and co., 1846.—3 v. : fronts., 8 plates, 11 maps (partly fold.).   **DA979.P24**

356.

Taylor, George, geographer, fl. 1778.

Taylor and Skinner's maps of the roads of Ireland, surveyed 1777 / [George Taylor and Andrew Skinner].—London : published for the authors; sold by G. Nicol, 1778.—xvi p., 288 p. of maps, 16 p.　　　**G1831.P2 T3 1778 <G&M : Vault>**

"A new & accurate map of the kingdom of Ireland," by Taylor & Skinner: fold. map inserted.

Names, Geographical

357.

Ainm : bulletin of the Ulster Place-Name Society.—Vol. 1 (1986)– .—Belfast : The Society, 1986–　　　**DA979.A37**

Ainm, devoted to the study of Irish names, is written chiefly in English, partly in Irish.

358.

General alphabetical index to the townlands and towns, parishes, and baronies of Ireland : based on the census of Ireland for the year 1851.—Baltimore : Genealogical Pub. Co., 1984.—968 p.　　　**DA979.G46 1984**

Originally published in Dublin and printed by A. Thom for H.M.S.O. in 1861.

359.

Goblet, Yann Morvran.

A topographical index of the parishes and townlands of Ireland in Sir William Petty's mss. barony maps (c. 1655–9) (Bibliotheque nationale de Paris, fonds anglais, nos. 1 & 2) and Hiberviae delineatio (c. 1672).—Dublin : Pub. by the Stationery office, 1932.—xx, 379, [1] p.　　　**DA979.G63**

360.

Joyce, P[atrick] W[eston], 1827–

The origin and history of Irish names of places.—4th ed.—Dublin : McGlashan & Gill, 1875.—2 v.　　　**DA920.J89**

Reprinted in Wakefield by E. P. Publishing in 1972 **(DA979.J7 1972)**.

361.

Room, Adrian.

A dictionary of Irish place-names / Adrian Room. Rev. ed.—Belfast: Appletree Press, c1994.—136 p.　　　**DA979.R67 1994**

Includes bibliographical references (p. 134–136).

Names,
Personal

362.
Bell, Robert, 1953–
The book of Ulster surnames / Robert Bell.—Belfast ; St. Paul,
Minn. : Blackstaff Press, 1988.—285 p.   **CS2415.B45 1988**
Bibliography: p. 258–259.

363.
Cairney, C. Thomas, 1958–
Clans and families of Ireland and Scotland : an ethnography of
the Gael, A.D. 500–1750 / by C. Thomas Cairney.—Jefferson,
N.C. : McFarland, c1989.—xii, 210 p. : ill. **DA927.C35 1989**
Bibliography: p. 197–203.

364.
Coghlan, Ronan.
Book of Irish names : first, family & place names / Ronan
Coghlan, Ida Grehan & P. W. Joyce.—New York : Sterling Pub.
Co., c1989.—128 p. : ill.   **DA979.C64 1989**

365.
De Breffny, Brian.
Irish family names : arms, origins, and locations / Brian de
Breffny.—Dublin : Gill and Macmillan, 1982.—192 p. : ill.
   CS2415.D43 1982
Bibliography: p. 191.

366.
Durning, William P.
The Scotch-Irish / William and Mary Durning ; editor,
Margaret Harris.—La Mesa, Calif. : Irish Family Names
Society, c1991.—iii, 184 p. : ill., maps.   **E184.S4 D87 1991**
Includes bibliographical references (p. 33–35).

367.
The Great families of Ireland.—Kansas City, Mo. : Irish
Genealogical Foundation, c1981.—16, 382 p. : ill.
   CS2415.G73 1981

368.
Grehan, Ida.
Pocket guide to Irish family names / Ida Grehan.—Belfast :
Appletree Press, c1985.—95 p. : ill.—(An Appletree pocket
book).   **CS2415.G74 1985**

369.

Kelly, Patrick, 1893–

Irish family names with origins, meanings, clans, arms, crests, and mottoes.—2nd ed.—[S.l., s.n.], 1958.—136 p.

CS2415.K4 1958

Reprinted in Detroit by Gale Research in 1976.

370.

McClelland, James.

Irish surnames and their possible locations for family history research / James McClelland.—Silverdale, NSW : J. McClelland Research ; Penrith, NSW : Distributed by K. Ainsworth, 1984.—2 v.—(James McClelland's Convict, pioneer, and immigrant series of Australia).   **CS484.M37 1984<fol.>**

371.

MacLysaght, Edward.

Irish families : their names, arms, and origins / Edward MacLysaght.—4th ed., rev. and enl.—Dublin : Irish Academic Press, 1985.—248 p. : ill. (some col.).   **CS2415.M235 1985**

372.

MacLysaght, Edward.

More Irish families / Edward MacLysaght.—Blackrock, Co. Dublin : Irish Academic Press, 1982.—254 p. : ill.

CS2415.M238 1982

"A new revised and enlarged edition of *More Irish Families,* incorporating Supplement to *Irish Families,* with an essay on Irish chieftainries."

373.

MacLysaght, Edward.

The surnames of Ireland.—6th ed.—Blackrock, Co. Dublin : Irish Academic Press, 1985.—xxi, 312 p : ill.

CS2415.M24 1985

Bibliography: p. xvii–xviii.

374.

Matheson, Robert E. (Robert Edwin), *Sir,* 1845–1926.

Special report on surnames in Ireland. Together with Varieties and synonymes of surnames and Christian names in Ireland.—Baltimore : Genealogical Pub. Co., 1968.—78, 94 p.

CS2415.M32 1968

Originally published in 1901 and 1909.

375.

Woulfe, Patrick.

Sloinnte Gaedheal is Gall : Irish names and surnames.—Dublin : M. H. Gill & son, ltd., 1923.—xlvi, 696 p.

Microfilm 83/5108 (CS) <MicRR>

Contents: Table of values of Irish letters—The Irish name-system—Names of men: English-Irish—Names of women: English-Irish—Surnames: English-Irish—Names of men: Irish-English—Names of women: Irish-English—Surnames: Irish-English—Appendix: Clan-names.

Reprinted in Baltimore by Genealogical Pub. Co. in 1967.

Periodicals

376.
The All-Ireland heritage.—Vol. 1, no. 1 (Feb. 1984)–[1994].—Vienna, Va. : D. R. H. Associates, c1984–[1994].   **CS480.A45**
Three times a year.

377.
Analecta Hibernica / Comisiún Láimhscríbhinní na hÉireann, The Irish Manuscripts Commission.—No. 1 (Mar. 1930)–.—Dublin : Stationery Office of Saorstát Éireann, 1930–
DA905.A3
Irregular.

378.
Association for the Preservation of the Memorials of the Dead in Ireland.
Journal.—Vol. 1 (1888)– .—Dublin : [s.n.], 1890– **DA900.A84**
Title varies.

379.
Familia / Ulster Genealogical & Historical Guild.—Vol. 2, no. 1 (1985)– .—Belfast : Ulster Historical Foundation, c1985–
CS440.F36

380.
Gaelic gleanings.—Vol. 1, no. 1 (Nov. 1981)– .—Santa Ana, Calif. : Magee Publications, 1981– **E184.I6 G33**
Quarterly.

381.
The Irish ancestor.—Vol. 1 (1969)–Vol. 16 (1984).—[Dublin : s.n., 1970–1984]. **CS480.I7**
Semi-annual.

382.
Irish Family History : Journal of the Irish Family History Society.—Vol. 1 (1985)– .—Tullamore, Ireland : The Society, [1985– **CS480.J68**
Annual.

383.
Irish family links.—Vol. 2, no. 1 (May 1984)– .—Belfast : Irish
Genealogical Association, [c1984–   **CS480.F34**
    Three times yearly.
    Continues *Family Links, Past and Present,* 1981–

384.
The Irish genealogist.—Began with Apr. 1937 issue.—
[London] : Irish Genealogical Research Society.   **CS480 .I7313**
    Official organ of the Irish Genealogical Research Society.

385.
Irish-American genealogist.—no. 8 (1977)– .—[Torrance, Calif.
: Augustan Society, 1977–].   **CS480.I72**
    Quarterly.

386.
The Journal of the American Irish Historical Society.—
Vol. 1 (1898/1919)–[Vol. 32 (1941)].—New York : The Society,
1898/1919–1941.   **E184.I6 A5**
    Excerpted and reprinted in part by Michael Joseph O'Brien
in *Irish Settlers in America : A Consolidation of Articles from the
Journal of the American Irish Historical Society.*   **(E184.I6 O26).**

387.
Walker's Hibernian magazine.—Dublin : Printed by R. Gibson,
[1771–1811].—41 v. in 49. : ill., plates, ports., maps, diagrs.
        AP3.W3 <Rare Bk. Coll. : Pre-1801 Coll>
    Marriages listed from 1771 to 1812 are indexed in Henry
Farrar's *Irish Marriages* (Baltimore, Genealogical Pub. Co., 1972.
532 p. **CS482.F3 1972**).

Religions ❧

388.
Church of Ireland.
    Directory.—(1968)– .—Dublin : Irish Church Publications,
    1968–   **BX5440.A3**
        Annual.

389.
Goodbody, Olive C.
    Guide to Irish Quaker records, 1654–1860 / by Olive C.
    Goodbody ; with contribution on Northern Ireland records by
    B. G. Hutton.—Dublin : Stationery Office for the Irish
    Manuscripts Commission, 1967.—237 p.

390.

A Guide to Irish churches and graveyards / compiled under the direction of Brian Mitchell.—Baltimore : Genealogical Pub. Co., c1990.—ix, 253 p. **CS481.G85 1990**

391.

A History of congregations in the Presbyterian Church in Ireland, 1610–1982.—Belfast : Presbyterian Historical Society of Ireland, 1982.—vi, 808 p. **BX9060.H54 1982**

392.

History of congregations of the Presbyterian Church in Ireland and biographical notices of eminent Presbyterian ministers and laymen, with the signification of names of places / with introduction and notes by W. D. Killen ; illustrated with portraits of Henry Cooke, J. S. Reid, and W. D. Killen.—Belfast : J. Cleeland ; Edinburgh : J. Gemmell, 1886.—viii, 290 p., [3] leaves of plates : ill. **BX9060.H55 1886**

393.

Hyman, Louis, 1912–

The Jews of Ireland : from earliest times to the year 1910.—Jerusalem : published jointly by the Jewish Historical Society of England, London and Israel Universities Press, 1972.—xix, 403 p. : ill. **DS135.I72 H88**

Bibliography: p. 352–366.

394.

Irish Catholic directory and diary.—(1960)– .—Dublin : J. Duffy and Co.,1960– **BX1503.A3 I6**

Annual.

Continues *Irish Catholic Directory and Almanac for. . . with complete directory in English* [1877–].

395.

Irish church records : their history, availability, and use in family and local history research / edited by James G. Ryan.—Glenageary, Co. Dublin : Flyleaf Press, 1992.—207 p. : ill., map. **CS496.C56 I75 1992**

396.

Lee, Grace Lawless.

The Huguenot settlements in Ireland.—London ; New York : Longmans, Green and co. [1936].—xi, 280, [2] p. : front. (map). **BX9456.I7 L4**

397.

Mitchell, Brian.

A guide to Irish parish registers / Brian Mitchell.—Baltimore : Genealogical Pub. Co., 1988.—xvii, 134 p.

CD1118.5.A1 M58 1988

398.

Reid, James Seaton, 1798–1851.

History of the Presbyterian church in Ireland, comprising the civil history of the province of Ulster, from the accession of James the First: with a preliminary sketch of the progress of the reformed religion in Ireland during the sixteenth century.—New ed.—Belfast : W. Mullan, 1867.—3 v.　　**BX9060.R4 1867**

Wills ☙

399.

Clare, Wallace.

Irish genealogical guides : a guide to copies & abstracts of Irish wills.—March, [Eng.] ; Priv. print. by Sharman & co., 1930.— 111 p.　　**CS482.C4**

Reprinted in Baltimore by Genealogical Pub. Co. in 1972.

400.

Ireland (Eire). Irish Manuscripts Commission.

Quaker records, Dublin : abstracts of wills / edited by P. Beryl Eustace and Olive C. Goodbody.—Dublin : Stationery Off., 1957.—vi, 136 p.　　**CS497.D8 I73 1957**

The wills are in the possession of the Dublin and Wexford Monthly Meetings of the Society of Friends.

401.

Phillimore, William Phillimore Watts, 1853–

Indexes to Irish wills.—London : Phillimore and co., 1909–1920.—5 v.　　**CS482.P6**

Contents: v. 1. Ossory, Leighlin, Ferms, Kildare—v. 2. Cork and Ross, Cloyne—v. 3. Cashel and Emily, Waterford and Lismore, Killaloe and Kilfenora, Limerick, Ardfert and Aghadoe—v. 4. Dromore, Newry, and Mourne—v. 5. Derry and Raphoe.

Reprinted in Baltimore by Genealogical Pub. Co. in 1970.

402.

Registry of Deeds (Ireland).

Abstracts of wills / edited by P. Beryl Eustace.—Dublin : Stationery Office, 1954–<1984>.—v. <1–3>.　　**CS482.R44 1954**

Contents: v. 1. 1708–1745—v. 2. 1746–1785—v. 3. 1785–1832.

403.

Vicars, Arthur Edward, *Sir,* 1864.

Index to the prerogative wills of Ireland, 1536–1810 / [edited by Sir Arthur Edward Vicars].—Dublin : E. Ponsonby, 1897.—ix p., 1 leaf, 512 p.   **Microfilm 8724 CS <MicRR>**

Reprinted in Baltimore by Genealogical Pub. Co. in 1967.

Emigration

404.

Adams, William Forbes.

Ireland and Irish emigration to the new world from 1815 to the famine.—New Haven : Yale University Press, 1932.—vii p., 1 leaf, 444 p.   **JV7711.Z79 N63**

Reprinted in New York by Russell & Russell in 1967 and in Baltimore by Genealogical Pub. Co. in 1980.

405.

Dickson, R. J.

Ulster emigration to colonial America, 1718–1775 / by R. J. Dickson.—London : Routledge & Kegan Paul, 1966.—xiv, 320 p. : map, tables.—(Ulster-Scot historical series ; no. 1).   **E184.S4 D47**

Bibliography: p. 298-311.

Reprinted in Belfast by the Ulster Historical Foundation in 1988.

406.

Emigrants from Ireland to America, 1735–1743 : a transcription of the report of the Irish House of Commons into enforced emigration to America / by Frances McDonnell.—Baltimore : Genealogical Pub. Co., c1992.—134 p.   **E184.I6 E45 1992**

From the *Journal of the House of Commons of the Kingdom of Ireland,* Vol. 7, 1796.

407.

The Famine immigrants : lists of Irish immigrants arriving at the port of New York, 1846–1851 / Ira A. Glazier, editor ; Michael Tepper, associate editor.—Baltimore : Genealogical Pub. Co., 1983–1986.—7 v.   **E184.I6 F25 1983**

Includes bibliographical references and indexes.

Contents: v. 1. January 1846–June 1847—v. 2. July 1847–June 1848—v. 3. July 1848–March 1849—v. 4. April 1849–September 1849—v. 5. October 1849–May 1850—v. 6. June 1850–March 1851—v. 7. April 1851–December 1851.

408.

Houston, Cecil J., 1943–

Irish emigration and Canadian settlement : patterns, links, and letters / Cecil J. Houston, William J. Smyth.—Toronto ; Buffalo : University of Toronto Press ; Belfast : Ulster Historica Foundation, c1990.—viii, 370 p. : ill.　　**F1035.I6 H68 1990**

Includes bibliographical references (p. [341]–364) and index.

409.

Irish passenger lists, 1847–1871 : lists of passengers sailing from Londonderry to America on ships of the J. & J. Cooke Line and the McCorkell Line / compiled under the direction of Brian Mitchell.—Baltimore : Genealogical Pub. Co., 1988.—xvii, 333 p. : ill.　　**E184.I6 I69 1988**

410.

Lockhart, Audrey.

Some aspects of emigration from Ireland to the North American colonies between 1660 and 1775 / Audrey Lockhart.—New York : Arno Press, 1976.—243 p.—(The Irish–Americans).　　**E184.I6 L65 1976**

Bibliography: p. 213–243.

Reprint of the author's thesis, Trinity College, Dublin, 1971.

411.

Miller, Kerby A.

Emigrants and exiles : Ireland and the Irish exodus to North America / Kerby A. Miller.—New York : Oxford University Press, 1985.—xii 684 p. : map.　　**JV7711.Z79 U55 1985**

Bibliography: p. 583–664.

412.

Mitchell, Brian.

Irish emigration lists, 1833–1839 : lists of emigrants extracted from the Ordnance Survey memoirs for Counties Londonderry and Antrim / compiled under the direction of Brian Mitchell.—Baltimore : Genealogical Pub. Co., c1989.—vii, 118 p., [2] p. of plates : ill.　　**CS497.L66 M58 1989**

413.

Schlegel, Donald M.

Passengers from Ireland : lists of passengers arriving at American ports between 1811 and 1817 / transcribed from the Shamrock or Hibernian Chronicle by Donald M. Schlegel.—Baltimore : Genealogical Pub. Co., 1980.—158 p.　**E184.I6 S34**

414.

The Search for missing friends : Irish immigrant advertisements placed in the Boston pilot / Ruth–Ann M. Harris and Donald M. Jacobs, editors ; B. Emer O'Keeffe, associate editor, Dominique M. Pickett, assistant editor.—Boston : New England Historic Genealogical Society, 1989–<1995>.—v. <1 –4 > : ill.   **F73.9.I6 S43 1989**

Includes bibliographical references and indexes.
Contents: v. 1. 1831–1850 —v. 2. 1851–1853—v. 3. 1854–1856—v. 4. 1857–1860.

Irish in America

415.
Considine, Robert Bernard, 1906–

It's the Irish.—[1st ed.]—Garden City, N.Y. : Doubleday, 1961.—274 p. : ill.   **E184.I6 C75**

416.
Fitzgerald, Margaret E.

The uncounted Irish in Canada and the United States / Margaret E. Fitzgerald and Joseph A. King.—Toronto : P. D. Meany Publishers, c1990.—xiv, 377 p. : ill.   **E184.I6 F58 1990**
Includes bibliographical references (p. 329–356) and index.

417.
Griffin, William D.

The book of Irish Americans / William D. Griffin.—1st ed.— New York : Times Books, c1990.—xii, 404 p. : ill.
E184.I6 G739 1990

418.
McGee, Thomas D'Arcy, 1825–1868.

A history of the Irish settlers in North America, from the earliest period to the census of 1850.—Baltimore : Genealogical Pub. Co., 1974.—240 p.   **E184.I6 M15 1974**
Reprint of the 1852 ed. which was published by P. Donaldson in Boston.
Includes bibliographical references.

419.
O'Brien, Michael Joseph, 1870–1960.

The Irish in America : immigration, land, probate, administration, birth, marriage, and burial records of the Irish in America in and about the eighteenth century / [edited by Michael J. O'Brien].—Baltimore : Genealogical Pub. Co., 1965.—63 p.
E184.I6 O25

420.

O'Brien, Michael Joseph, 1870–1960.

Irish settlers in America : a consolidation of articles from the Journal of the American Irish Historical Society / by Michael J. O'Brien ; indexed by Thomas L. Hollowak.—Baltimore : Genealogical Pub. Co., 1979.—2 v. E184.I6 O26

421.

O'Brien, Michael Joseph, 1870–1960.

Pioneer Irish in New England / by Michael J. O'Brien, LL.D.—New York : P.J. Kenedy & sons, [c1937].—xiv, 15–325 p. F15.I6 O3

422.

O'Connell, J. C.

The Irish in the revolution and the civil war, (rev. and enl.) embracing the Spanish-American and Philippine wars and every walk of life.—Washington : The Trades Unionist Press, 1903.—110 p. E184.I6 O3

423.

O'Laughlin, Michael C.

Irish settlers on the American frontier.—Kansas City, Mo. : Irish Genealogical Foundation, [c1984–].—v. <1 > : ill.

F596.3.I6 O43 1984

Contents: v. 1. 1770–1900, gateway west through Missouri.

424.

The Untold story : the Irish in Canada / edited by Robert O'Driscoll & Lorna Reynolds.—Toronto : Celtic Arts of Canada, 1988.—2 v. (xxxii, 1041 p.) : ill. (some col.).

F1035.I6 U57 1988

Includes bibliographies and index.

425.

Wittke, Carl Frederick 1892–

The Irish in America.—Baton Rouge : Louisiana State University Press, [c1956].—xi, 319 p. E184.I6 W5

Bibliography: p. 295–306.

Reprinted in New York by Russell & Russell in 1970.

Author and Title Index
(The numbers refer to entries, not pages.)

J Jack, R. Ian, 238
Jackson, Ronald Vern, 94
Jacobs, Donald M., 414
Jacobs, Phyllis M., 49
James, Alwyn, 103
Jenkins, Geraint H., 242
Jenkins, R. T., 245
The Jews of Ireland, 393
Johnson, Gordon, 104
Johnston, James Brown, 148
Jones, Francis, 232, 256
Jones, Henry Z., 301
Jones, Nansi C., 257
Jones, Philip Henry, 239
The Journal of the American Irish Historical Society, 386
Journal of the Association for the Preservation of the Memorials of the Dead in Ireland, 378
Joyce, P. W., 345, 364
Joyce, Patrick Weston, 360
Judd, Michael, 62
The Judges in Ireland, 1221–1921, 321

K *Kalendars of Gwynedd*, 253
Kaminkow, Marion J., 31
Karras, Alan L., 215
Keating, Geoffrey, 1570?–1644?, 302
Kelly, Patrick, 369
Key to the Parochial Registers of Scotland, 120
Killen, W.D., 392
Kitzmiller, John Michael, 13

Lachman, David C., 168
Lairds, Bard, and Mariners, 218
Lamb, John Alexander, 172
Land Owners in Ireland, 337
Landsman, Ned C., 216
Lart, Charles Edmund, 95
Lasker, Gabriel Ward, 78, 265
Lee, Grace Lawless, 396
Lee, Sidney, 48
Leet, Ambrose, 348
Lehmann, William Christian, 217
LeRoy, Bruce, 218
Lester, DeeGee, 312
Letters Written by John O'Donovan..., 317
Lewis, Samuel, 69, 143, 258, 349–350
Lewis's Atlas Comprising the Countries of Ireland..., 349
Lhuyd, Edward, 1660–1709, 243
Limbus Patrum Marganifl et Glamorganifl, 228
List of Wills, Administrations, etc., 99
A List of Works Relating to Scotland, 117
Livingstone, M., 124
Lloyd, Jacob Youde William, 233
Lloyd, John Edward, 245
Lloyd, John Edward, *Sir*, 244
Llyfr Baglan, 235